Advance Praise for *No Surrender*

"Patrick Bisher's story of overcoming adversity as a child and then as a Navy SEAL is inspiring, riveting and informative. Patrick's story and lessons will inspire everyone and should be read by all. As a retired brigadier general with combat experience in Afghanistan, I was riveted by Patrick's grit and perseverance and humbled by his never give up attitude. A must read!"

–**Anthony Tata**, Brigadier General U.S. Army (Ret.),
commanded combat units in the 82nd & 101st Airborne and the
10th Mountain Division, and bestselling author

"I couldn't put it down. A memoir that reads like a thriller, and a real-life hero who pushes through unimaginable obstacles. *No Surrender* is not only an aptly-named book, it's also a winner."

–**Grant Blackwood**, #1 *New York Times* bestselling author
and former Navy Operations Specialist & Pilot Rescue Swimmer

"It was an honor to be given the first few chapters of Patrick Bisher's book. Having had the honor to serve with the SEALs myself, I can say that Patrick epitomizes the SEAL Ethos. Unlike the 'tell-all' books of late, Patrick Bisher's inspiring story sends a positive message of how one man can overcome anything through faith and integrity. From crippled boy to Navy SEAL, to injured Team Guy and back again to his unit, Patrick's story is one of perseverance, tenacity and triumph and how determination and faith can overcome all obstacles. Expertly told with the help of bestselling author Jon Land, I have no doubt this book with be an instant success and will touch and change many lives."

–**Jeffrey Wilson**, former Navy SEAL chief trauma surgeon,
Naval officer, and award-winning author

"*No Surrender* is a true story of perseverance, and overcoming huge obstacles all while keeping a never quit/never give up attitude. The same mental toughness exhibited at age 9, got Patrick through SEAL training as a grown man. As a former SEAL Sniper, I am humbled by this man's story and it will inspire anyone who reads it."

–**Dr. Howard Wasdin**, former Navy SEAL sniper

NO SURRENDER

FAITH, FAMILY, AND FINDING YOUR WAY

Patrick Bisher

with Jon Land

A POST HILL PRESS BOOK

No Surrender:
Faith, Family, and Finding Your Way
© 2017 by Patrick Bisher
All Rights Reserved

ISBN: 978-1-68261-300-9
ISBN (eBook): 978-1-6826130-1-6

Interior Design and Composition by Greg Johnson, Textbook Perfect

Post Hill Press
New York and Nashville
posthillpress.com

Printed in the United States of America

DEDICATION

This book is dedicated to my family... To my wife, who keeps me from falling too far down or going too far without my lifeline. You are the one who saved me on this earth, you are the one who keeps me out of trouble when my tongue could whip. I was the wild beast and you are the only one that could bring me back to Christ, and back to what we have now. You are my lighthouse when I am the ship in the storm. I'll love you forever.

My kids, you are very special in your own way. Never feel like you have to live a life like mine or follow in my footsteps. Nothing would make me prouder than for you to take the wisdom God has given us through his living word and apply it to your life, and not do what I did! I am always here for you and will always be encouraging for you to reach your dreams and find your path in life.

The men who have paid the ultimate sacrifice for this country, and those who continue to answer our nation's call in this time of divisions within our nation. For my brothers who go to work every day not knowing what will happen next. Your courage to preserve what others have paved for us, and your continued pursuit of defending those who are unable to defend themselves leaves me awestruck.

To the brotherhood, thank you for giving me something to belong to and be proud to be a part of. You turned me into a man, and then into a warrior, and then something even more. I will always be in your service and do my best to uphold the oath and the SEAL ethos until my last breath.

Mom and Dad, there is not a day that goes by that I am not grateful for everything you have sacrificed for me and our whole family. Your life is a testimony of how to live a life as we are commanded. You have always shown me what pure love is. I hope that I can be like you and keep our traditions going for generations.

CONTENTS

ACKNOWLEDGMENTS

Cassidy Bisher for being able to push me into a dream world that became my reality. You gave me a reason to believe in myself, without your words and actions to tell me to jump, I would have never been able to soar like and eagle.

The SEAL Teams and the Navy for allowing me to be a part of your brotherhood, and teaching me the life lessons that I can now give back to others in this life.

Joe Sweeney, for showing me how to approach life and business in the real world with your mentorship and your two books Networking is a Contact Sport, and Moving the Needle.

Erik Spolstra for thinking outside the box and allowing me to help you and your team from a different perspective.

Jeff Wilson for introduction me to everyone you did even though it did nothing for you. Thank you for your friendship and help with the book.

Jon Land.... Need I say more, than to merely speak your name? You speak Bisher fluently, and gave up your thoughts and your vision to see the real purpose of my book and its message. Thank you for not trying to write the book and seeing the diamond in the dirt.

And a great team that has supported the efforts to see his book through to publication from agent Bob Diforio, to Post Hill Press publisher Anthony Ziccardi, along with Billie Brownell, Gavin Carruthers and a great editor in Jon Ford who made my job that much easier.

Lastly Pat, Brendan, Kevin, Brett, Seth. You will always push me to be better than I am today. You will always drive me to be more than just what I am now. I will never forget our time and our friendships. I will never take this life for granted and will try my best to honor you in every way I can.

Please support the Navy SEAL foundation by donating today at:

TheNavySEALfoundation.org
The Honor foundation at thehonorfoundation.org

To contact me and support this cause or have any questions reach me at:

@PatrickBisher on Twitter
PatrickBisher.Consulting@gmail.com

A NOTE FROM PATRICK BISHER

This isn't a tall tale or a book where I save the universe and kill all the bad guys. I'm not writing a story about my missions as a Navy SEAL, or to shine the spotlight on me, or lie about what I have done. I have no interest in dishonoring the oath I took when I began the journey to become a Team Guy.

I'm sharing with you the fact that being counted as down and out, or being picked last in kickball, or told you would never walk again doesn't mean you have to accept the fate that others choose for you. You can do what I have done and prove others wrong about what's possible and what can be achieved in the process. You, like me, have the ability within you to overcome all things through what you already have inside you, something that's more powerful than you have ever imagined.

My life is a living testimony that through the most extreme adversity, great things can happen and something of a brotherhood can be found, like the one I found during the rigorous training of BUD/S (Basic Underwater Demolition/SEAL), training ground to become a Navy SEAL. You can find something to belong to, and you can find a place that gives you peace even through extreme anguish or racking pain, both physical and mental, as well as emotional.

My intention is to show that you can be anything you want to be. I want you to see that the struggle to survive is hard, and that to come out on top and reach your dreams is only achievable through a relentless desire to succeed. I know that if you have a dream that's big enough, the scope of reality and the obstacles in your way will pale by comparison. This is only possible by setting goals both small and large to reach what others see as impossible.

I want you to see how I've found a place where being a part of something really matters. We all feel lost sometimes in so many ways, and I wrote this book to help you find yourself during those times. To help you find what I did when I felt lost, by joining a true brotherhood and building the relationships that changed my life.

I want everyone to have what I have, to know what I know. For everyone who reads this book to understand the love and the bond of true friendship. I know there is no greater love than that of a brother who will lay down his life for yours. This brotherhood and bond that I found with the Navy SEALs is so great that it will never be broken by anyone or anything. Not any evil, death, or sin can change that. And I want those of you who feel left out, or believe that there's no way out, to see that there is a place, and a way, for you to belong.

I had to be willing to let go of my own personal desires for material success and change the way I thought to truly find what was missing for me. And in the process I became a part of something bigger than myself. I learned to change from the inside out. I needed to drop the old me that was fighting the world, stop being a victim and blaming everyone else for my problems. I had to develop a mindset dominated by positive thinking and learn to focus on the good in order to fight the bad, and win a war that for me was both literal and figurative.

I want you to know you can do that too, and I want to show you how. Our journeys will be different, but our destinations the same. I learned that life itself is a battlefield long before I fought for this country on an actual one. As you're about to see, throughout my life, long before I became a SEAL, I've had to fight my own battles to survive, including one against a degenerative bone disease as a boy that almost left me permanently disabled. The adversity I've faced may be less or more than what you've overcome or are in the process of facing now. Either way, I want to share with you the lessons I've learned along the way, lessons that have never come easily, in the hope that you'll find something in my journey that helps you on yours. Consider this my road map to happiness and fulfillment, and hopefully my words will serve as your guide.

Patrick

A hero is no braver than an ordinary man,
but he is brave five minutes longer.

–Ralph Waldo Emerson

PROLOGUE

Heroes

Iraq, September 2011

"Coming in hot! We're under pursuit!"

The distress call came in mid-morning from an Army Special Forces ODA (Operational Detachment Alpha, or "A Team"), just after my team had gotten back from the previous day's mission that had lasted eighteen straight hours. The Special Forces A Team was being chased by a much larger enemy convoy and evasive maneuvers were failing. We were the closest backup to their location a few miles east of us, meaning we might be their only hope.

"Let's go!" said our Officer in Charge (OIC). "Gear up!"

Only four of us were awake at the time, having just finished breakfast, but there was no time to rally the rest of the team. The four of us got our gear back on, set up our vehicle, and less than five minutes after getting the call we were speeding down the road to save our brothers no matter what it took.

There was nothing but sun-washed flat ground on either side of us, the possibility of IEDs planted on the roadside a persistent, looming threat. Not too many days before, a soldier was killed driving over the very spot we were about to pass, something that stuck with me and brought home in a stark way the reality of what we were facing. On this morning we faced another threat in the sandstorms building to the north, threatening to swallow us as we raced to the rescue.

I was manning the .50-caliber gun, exposed in the turret beneath finch-like birds circling overhead as if wondering what we were doing there. I could hear the occasional garble crackling over the radio in the cabin below, more contact from the Army Special Forces troops, but the loud surge of air rushing past the exposed turret kept me from hearing any specifics.

As I caught my first glimpse of the low-slung buildings comprising the city in southern Iraq near the Iranian border to which the Special Forces guys were headed, a nasty smell hit me at the same time. There were three rivers ahead, all of them teeming with raw sewage starting to bake under the building heat of the sun. I stayed ready on the .50, my hands sweating inside my gloves and the gun oil battling the thick, sour stench for control of my nostrils.

Never mind this wasn't our mission set. My leadership made a call to help others because our help was needed. No ifs, ands, or buts.

Simple as that.

What being a hero looks like to others and what it is to actually be a hero are two completely different things, our sensibilities warped by the background music and super-heated action in movies and television. The heroes that I know battle with the pain and the fear of losing their loved ones, of never getting the chance to see their wives again, watch their kids grow up or take their first steps. The heroes I know do everything they can for others without expecting anything in return. The heroes I know would give up their lives for mine, carry me ten miles up a mountain if that's what it took. I was with my heroes every day, serving beside them and counting on them, just as they counted on me.

Being a hero sucks the life right out of you at times, because you stare at evil and evil stares back. You look everything that others are trying desperately to stay away from square in the face. My heroes have lost eyes, legs, and lives, because glory wounds you to the core. What others may see as glorious, I can tell you firsthand it is bittersweet at best, especially when you're rolling straight into a sandstorm having no idea what awaits you on the other side.

But someone has to stand up against this evil. Someone who's capable of staring evil in its face and confronting it head on. I saw enough of that evil to last a lifetime, and it cost three of my closest friends their lives. Their names were Brendan Looney, Pat Feeks, and Kevin Ebbert, and I think about them every day. Maybe wherever they are now, they think about me too. About their brother who never should've made it this far, who'd been told as a nine-year-old boy he'd never walk again, and years later, that his ruined hip needed to be replaced. I miss them now as much as ever and feel privileged I had the opportunity to call them brothers.

Especially privileged, because I was lucky to have been deployed and lucky to just be walking, when for a large part of my life neither of those outcomes seemed possible. But I wasn't thinking about that as we raced to the rescue of our Army brothers, any more than I was thinking of the accident that had nearly ended my military career before it even started.

I was thinking that I had a job to do and nothing was going to stop me from doing it, as we picked up the pace toward our Army brothers who desperately needed us.

THE BOY

CHAPTER 1

Leg Braces

Lansing, Michigan; July 1991

"You'll never be able to walk again."

At first, I didn't think I heard my new doctor correctly. What nine-year-old boy could possibly imagine getting such news? The doctor was long faced and slightly balding. He seemed to be dulled by what he was saying because of how many people he had seen before me that day. It was late, around six-thirty in the evening.

It was the look on the doctor's face and the way my mother was squeezing my hand that told me I'd heard him right. I looked down at my legs, hating how my own body had betrayed me. Wouldn't let me play sports, run around, or play with my friends.

And now even walking was going to be denied to me.

The doctor told me I had developed a rare hip disease that had destroyed the hip bone and the socket. Back then, there was no sure surgical way to fix what was wrong with me. A normal life was out of the question.

My mother was working in the ER as a nurse in the same hospital at the time and she'd already gone to a coworker, who was an X-ray technician, to get his read on my films. His face immediately went blank.

"Julie, I can't tell you. I'm not allowed to say a thing. You need to wait to speak with the doctor."

So going into that meeting, she had reason to suspect something was very wrong. In fact, given her experience I expect she'd been fearing the truth for some time.

A few months back she'd noticed I was favoring my left leg and that I was limping badly; I overheard her mentioning it to my dad in a conversation when I was trying to keep up with my older brother on the beach during a trip to Florida. I'd come home from that trip to visit our extended family with severe pain in my left leg. I kept complaining about it to my mom and dad; it hurt so much to move it, that I had to stop going to karate which, given my devotion to my training, was a definite indicator that something was really wrong. Sure enough, after about a month of stretching and waiting for the leg to get better on its own, we went to the pediatrician who referred us to a specialist.

"You'll never be able to walk again."

The specialist and surgeon, Dr. Robert N. Hensinger, was warm-hearted, well mannered, and soft spoken. A gentle man out of the University of Michigan who I'd later learn was a true expert in these kind of pediatric orthopedic issues. The one who got the calls no one else wanted to take. He was the one who delivered the bad news around 6:30 that evening and went on to describe to me how my life was about to change forever. The best I could hope for was severely limited mobility, thanks to leg braces that could potentially become a permanent fixture for me if things didn't improve.

His words were like a dagger to my heart, my childhood seeming to end in that precise moment. The room felt cold and the scent of alcohol suddenly seemed stronger. The stale smells of the hospital started to creep their way into my skin and seemed to push me down even deeper into my chair. Prepared for this conversation, the doctor brought out the leg braces, comprised of metal, plastic, and Velcro, that I'd have to wear if I wanted any semblance of life at all.

4

Which to a nine-year-old boy didn't seem like much of one.

The doctor said there was no guarantee the leg braces would work, but we could hope for the best. Then he pulled out a pair of crutches and told me I'd be using them as well. I couldn't put any pressure on my left leg at all; that meant no walking, jumping, or even sitting the way I used to. I'd have to use my right leg for everything.

Yeah, right, I thought, with typically youthful indignation and denial. *Sure.*

I'd walked in here on my own and I'd walk myself right out the same way to show him how wrong he was. But I remained seated. The doctor said the only time I would be out of the leg braces was for the physical therapy sessions I'd need to keep my muscles from developing atrophy. My left leg had already weakened and looked puny in comparison to my right. The difference seemed even more striking in that moment.

"How about we give these a try?"

Without waiting for me to respond, Doctor Hensinger strapped the leg braces to both my legs and my waist, making them a part of me for the first time. He backed up from the chair and told me to stand up.

I tried to rise, but the braces held my legs at an awkward angle, keeping them spread apart. I felt as if I were riding a horse.

The crutches came next.

The doctor handed them over and showed me how to walk using them with my legs kept wide, thanks to the braces that felt like somebody had wrapped me in sheet metal. It was hard to walk, move, sit, stand, sleep—everything. Especially going up stairs. Stairs were the hardest.

I ended up practicing at home until I found the knack and got it right. It took a long time, but I felt like I'd really accomplished something. Call it a small victory, the best I could hope for at that point.

Then I began to develop painful blisters around my waist because of the straps. Underneath my arms, too, thanks to all the pressure on the crutches. At my next appointment, the doctor explained it was normal.

Normal? For who?

In time, he explained, blisters would come and eventually it would turn to callus. It would just take a while.

Funny how it didn't take long at all for people, especially other kids, to start staring at me. Every time I went to school or to the store or attending my older brother's sporting events, people were always staring. Whispering and shaking their heads. They'd look at me like I was a leper or somebody with something contagious that they didn't want to catch. And lots of times the people who didn't stare or shake their heads would come up and talk to me very slowly or loudly, as if I didn't know or understand what they were talking about. Mentally disabled too, I guess they thought.

"Mommy, look at that boy."

"Don't stare."

"But what's wrong with him?"

"Shhhhhhhhhhhhh..."

Typical of the conversations I overheard and never got used to. The words and the stares stuck with me, burned into my brain. They hurt so much, making it impossible for me to fully adapt to my plight. Because no matter how good I'd gotten at getting around on the crutches, or growing used to the leg braces, those words and stares served as a constant reminder that I wasn't normal and might never be again.

I wanted to turn and yell at them that I *was* normal. But then I'd look down at my legs and realize I wasn't. I shouldn't have blamed them, might've behaved the same way if it was some other kid in leg braces instead of me. I can't tell you how much I wanted to rip those braces off and fling them as far as I could by the straps. And whenever I went out in public, my feelings ended up hurting more than my legs. But that was okay because those who shunned me didn't realize how strong I was becoming. All those times somebody looked at me funny, or pointed, or whispered, I got stronger because I got angry. And being angry made me, more than anything else, want to prove that I was normal. I desperately didn't want to be disabled anymore, but as long as I was I'd never let it or them get the better of me. I pushed past the pain I was enduring and refused to let it show. Fueled myself with a burning desire not to be disabled anymore. That's the great thing about being a kid: you still believe in miracles.

But not for long.

After fourteen months of being on the crutches and in my leg braces, I went back for my regular three-month checkup. The doctor told me my condition was still worsening and the long-term prognosis was even more dire. Surgery was the only option now.

"Will I get cured?" I asked him.

"There are no guarantees. And it's risky."

"Risky?" I asked, swallowing hard.

"It's an experimental procedure," my mother explained.

I remember the phrase "subpar success rate." Maybe my mother mentioned it. More likely I overheard it the same way I overheard people whispering when I hobbled past them on my crutches.

"We'll think about it," my mother said to the doctor, supporting me as always. Figuratively and literally.

There wasn't much to think about. I didn't want to be stuck in leg braces for the rest of my life, and this might be the only chance I'd ever get to shed them. Even if that meant the very real risk of ending up bedridden or wheelchair-bound for the rest of my life.

"I want to do the surgery," I told my parents.

A few weeks later, in November of 1992, I checked into the hospital to have the operation. It was the first time I was ever anesthetized and I remember how blissful everything felt for those few moments before I surrendered my precarious hold on consciousness. It was like the happy dreams in which I could still walk without braces and crutches. Or pain. I could run again and be a normal kid playing with my friends, instead of a disabled boy looking out the window at other boys my age cruising by on the bicycles I had taken for granted, just like I'd taken everything for granted.

I woke up after the surgery in the recovery room with no idea where I was. Like a dream again, only a bad one accompanied by pangs of nausea. I looked around but it was so dark. I saw something that looked like a sheet, a drape hanging from the ceiling all the way around my bed. The only opening I noticed was on the left side of my bed to a window that provided a sliver of light to cut through the darkness. I tried to sit up but I was stuck. My legs, my torso, seemed cemented to the bed.

I'm paralyzed, I thought and felt a surge of fear that woke me up a little more, and that's when I remembered I was in the hospital. I listened to the steady beep of the machine with the cold fluid from the IV hooked to my arm. I braced myself with my arms to prop my head up. I ran my hands down over the cold roughness that surrounded my legs and chest and suddenly I remembered.

I was waking from hip surgery, and the heaviness I felt was due to a cast that covered my entire left leg up just past the hip, stopping about even with my stomach. So heavy it felt like the whole bed was going to crash through the floor from the weight. I started to sweat, cold beads that began to drip over my body, making my skin feel moist and clammy. I turned my head all the way over past the window and saw my mom sitting in a chair at my bedside. She looked like she was sleeping, but as soon as I made a sound, her eyes burst open.

"How long was I out for?" I asked, my voice dry and cracking.

"Six and a half hours. You're in the ICU, and you're going to be here awhile until they know you'll be okay."

"How long is that?"

My mother shrugged.

The nausea from the anesthesia replaced the terror of being unable to move. I was throwing up every ten minutes for hours. The vomit turned into nothing but neon yellow acid and it burned all the way from my stomach to my mouth. Because I couldn't sit up, my mom and I developed a code phrase to alert her when the next wave was coming. I'd manage to moan, "Oh, no," so she could quickly grab a trash bin and spare me the misery of vomiting on myself. I just turned my head and the warmth flowed over my cheek like lava.

The nausea lasted for a day or so, abating finally around the same time the doctor came back in to see us. We had no idea what to expect. I was so nervous, I was shaking. Was he going to tell me I'd be spending the rest of my life in a wheelchair? He didn't actually say much at all, just that I was now stable enough to go home. He explained that since I was in the full-body cast, an ambulance was the best option to get me there.

I'll never forget the look on my mother's face. It was a combination of terror and anxiety all squeezed into her eyes and brows. I knew an ambulance was out of the question, because we couldn't afford that type of luxury. So I told my mother that I didn't need the ambulance. She could take me home in a wheelbarrow, if it meant getting out of the hospital.

"I think we can do better than that," she said, managing a smile.

"Maybe an Amish buggy, Mom."

Her face seemed to relax some and she gave me a little smile. I didn't want her to feel any pain emotionally because of all that had to be done for me now, stuff I used to do for myself. My parents were already doing everything they could for me. They spent thousands of dollars and sacrificed so much to help me. They'd already lost one son to leukemia, something we didn't talk about much if at all, and everyone was scared. I wanted to make sure they knew I could handle it, that I was stronger than they thought I was.

That's when my mother gave our family friend Karen a call and arranged the pickup. Karen had a big, roomy van that I could comfortably ride in, which was good because I was ready to get the heck out of the hospital. Three days was long enough for me to be stuck in one room, although I wasn't giving much thought at that point to the fact that it could very well turn into an apt description of the rest of my life.

When it was time to leave, four people had to lift me out of the bed because the cast was so massive and I couldn't move in it. They eased me from the bed to a reclined wheelchair. Being rolled outside into the cold, brisk, wintery chill with a hint of snow in the air was a total shock, giving way to a painful ride home. Every bump we hit made me feel as if I had been jabbed by a knife in my leg.

It was great to be home, such a relief, but I was still stuck in bed. Same as the hospital, only more familiar. And my parents had to flip me over so I wouldn't get bedsores on my butt, just like the nurses had done.

I couldn't go to school and I really didn't want to because the mammoth cast embarrassed me, made me feel like the helpless cripple I'd already been teased about when I had my braces and crutches. I spent my days in the living room, rotating every few hours from my back to my front again so I wouldn't get bedsores. If I needed help or had to go to the bathroom, my mom gave me an old antique cowbell to ring so that I could call her.

One day maybe a month into my recovery I dropped the bell from the bed that had been placed for me in first floor living room, and it landed on a pillow on the floor. Man, I had to poop so badly! So I did what anyone else would try to do: get up enough to reach for the bedpan that was at the end of the bed toward my feet. I managed to slide to the edge of the bed and used my hands and arms to hold myself up using the couch and the bed, just as I would with crutches. But my left foot was fully cast all the way down to my toes and I had no traction, so I slipped and slid past the end of the bed, and the bedpan fell on the floor.

Oh boy...

I looked the other way with anger, only to see the bathroom. A real toilet! If I could make it through the dining room and to the hall

I could get there, never having imagined such a simple act would gain such monumental importance. It did, though, because this was something that I hadn't done in over six weeks.

That's it! I said to myself. *I'm going to do this!*

So I slid and crawled and slithered my way to the bathroom toilet. Twenty-five minutes later I was there, twenty-five minutes to cover all of twenty feet. I felt like the king of the world, rewarded with the best poop I ever had! It was also the best I'd felt in weeks, maybe months, given that it had been so long since I'd accomplished anything of note.

And that trip across the first floor of my house was a big deal, believe me. We all take the little, most humdrum things for granted until we can't do them anymore. I was starting to learn the lesson of finding solace in small victories and pleasures, crucial to recovering from such a serious operation or any major setback in life. I was learning that lesson the hard way as a boy instead of a man. And I carried it with me for years, all the way up to and through my training to become a Navy SEAL.

Maybe that day crawling and pushing myself across the floor was actually my first day of SEAL training, now that I think of it.

After I was done, however, I took a look at the distance I traveled and knew I needed to get back in that bed in the living room before my mom got there or else I was going to be in *big* trouble. After twenty minutes I was totally fatigued. I just lay down on the hardwood floor, hoping to gain back some strength before it was too late.

Just then, my mom walked in and saw me on the floor.

"What's this? What happened?" she asked, looking more concerned than angry.

"I had to go to the bathroom. Don't get mad."

"Did you hurt yourself?"

"No."

"Then I'm not mad. But don't even think about doing it again," she said, positioning herself to hoist me back into my customary spot.

Things went on uneventfully, until one day when my mom was washing my hair with the sink sprayer, because I couldn't take a shower or get my body cast wet. She leaned me over a little too much to get the shampoo out of my hair, and I slipped back off the wheelchair. My legs went straight up in the air, and she let out a loud scream as my head fell right into our dog's water dish. She looked at me, worried that I'd been hurt.

I just looked at her and said, "Well, at least my hair is washed!"

And we both smiled.

I didn't want my mom and dad to know how lousy I felt being cooped up all the time with no company other than the television. I figured they'd been through enough, having already lost one child, and neither complaining nor self-pity was going to help any of us. So whenever they asked how I was feeling, I always said fine and, more to the point, that I was improving even though it seldom felt that way when I couldn't even move from my chest to my toes.

I attended school from my bed. My friends brought over my schoolwork so I didn't fall behind, but they never stayed long. I had an in-home teacher come in to make sure I was doing what I was supposed to. I hated the whole process. It was like doing homework all the time and I felt detached from the world, a prisoner. I began to lose interest in my schoolwork, along with any desire to learn anything. It was like the cast was holding my mind hostage as well, again giving me new appreciation for even more of the things I'd always taken for granted—yes, like school. And being able to play with my friends, or jumping on my bike, and riding to the park or playground.

I couldn't jump anymore, or ride. Or even walk for that matter.

I only paid attention to the subjects of English and history, because they interested me and even took my mind off my misery. As the weeks passed, I lost interest in those too, and being trapped in a cast, lying on a hospital bed in the living room, consumed all my thoughts. I started counting the days until the cursed thing would come off, then moved to hours and minutes. And, after two more months of being a prisoner in my own body, I went back to the hospital to get my cast off. I imagined them telling me I was healed, could picture the saw cutting through the now rank plaster to free me to live my life again.

Well, that didn't happen.

A technician sawed off the cast in two pieces. When it came off, he found a few markers, some pencils, and a couple other things that I had pushed down inside to reach an itch. I took a look at my leg and lost my breath; it looked like a mummy in its sarcophagus. Yellow and crusty and my hairs were long and it looked like all of my muscles had withered away. It didn't look like a leg, mine or anybody else's. It looked like it belonged on a corpse.

The nurses and the physician's assistant took a washcloth and washed my leg to rid me of the stench that had settled in after so many weeks. I tried to lift my leg to move it up and out of the bottom half of the cast, but found I couldn't move it at all.

I was no stranger to pain, of course, but this was different because I'd let myself believe I'd been somehow magically healed. That the surgery, and the cast, had made me whole and normal again. But the pain was so bad I couldn't stop wincing and grimacing. In that moment, I faced the real and even likely possibility that this was going to be my life. Always in pain, thanks to a leg that would never be anything more than a dead weight. I'd had so many dreams before, all of them replaced by a single dream of being normal again. Right then, even that dream was dashed.

I'll never forget that moment. Both of my parents had been able to get off work, filled with the same expectations I was, and now their palpable disappointment matched mine. It couldn't get any worse.

Then the doctor came in and it did.

"Things didn't progress as we'd hoped," he said, surprising none of us.

My parents and I waited for him to go on.

"You're going to need to use crutches and put absolutely no weight or pressure on the leg for six more months."

"And then what?" I managed to ask, through the thick clog that had formed in my throat.

"You're going to be better, fine."

"Are you sure this time?"

"No, but I'm optimistic. We're going to need to perform a second surgery..."

Second surgery? Had I heard him right?

"...in which we transplant some of the bone marrow from your right leg to your left. Our hope is it'll form a solid bone structure that's not there now and stop the deterioration process of the femur."

Second surgery, I repeated in my mind again, choking back tears.

"How long?"

I could tell he wanted to give me something more concrete, more reason for real hope than he was able to. "We won't know until a few months go by."

That was the best he could do.

What You Can Learn from This...

1. The road to success is long and arduous. If I focused on the big picture, I would lose heart and would have my doubts, but if I focused on the small tasks one step at a time, things were manageable. I had to set up short-term goals to reach long-term success.

2. I realized I was different; I was not "normal." Everyone feels different at some point in time; we are all different. That is what makes us unique.

3. We all know life is not fair, it never will be. Learn to deal with it. Don't blame others for the circumstances you are in; instead, change your attitude. What are you going to do about it? The old saying goes, "If God gives you lemons...then make lemonade."

CHAPTER 2

A Boy's Life

Lansing, Michigan; 1992

A few days after getting home from the second operation that put me back on crutches, I got up off my couch and crutched outside. The mere act of standing up was agonizing, my leg feeling like I was moving a piece of dead meat around. I made it outside and saw my mother reading in a chair, drinking her homemade, unsweetened iced tea.

She almost spilled it when she saw me. "What are you doing outside?"

"The doctor told me I was allowed to get up."

"Get up," she repeated firmly. "That doesn't mean walking around."

So inside again I went, back to life on the couch for six more months. I thought about crossing the days off on a calendar, but the very notion of having so many pages to flip made that process seem way too depressing. I had to continue to do my schoolwork from home. The leg braces were off, the cast was off, but I still had my crutches and was under severe restrictions regarding my mobility, as my mother had aptly pointed out.

Put absolutely no weight or pressure on the leg, the doctor had instructed. And I guess I'd tried to find wiggle room in his order where none existed.

By this point, after so long, I'd let myself believe I'd be back to normal, but it felt as if I was even further back than ever and going in the wrong direction. Sitting on the couch a few days after I'd dared venture outside, I began to notice that the pain around the incision and the scar was gone. That got better quickly, but the pain in my hip didn't. Three times every day, I went through the physical therapy workouts I'd been given to help get that skinny leg back to normal.

I began to question God and asked Him why He would let something like this happen to me? I was a good kid, wasn't I? Wallowing in youthful self-pity, I began fixating on all the things I'd done that I might never be able to do again. Before the diagnosis, I was the fastest kid in school. I was good at sports and karate, once so much a part of my life but now shrouded in memories from what seemed like a long, long time ago.

After the prescribed six-month regimen, my hip was still throbbing and achy all the time. But the doctor said I could start walking again and told me only time would tell the extent of my recovery.

How much more time? I wanted to ask him, desperate for answers I knew he couldn't give me.

The only person who could supply those answers was me. It was up to me now, me and nobody else. It hurt to walk, every step a challenge, but I began disciplining myself to use the crutches less and less. A month after getting the cast removed, I was getting up to grab a snack, go to the bathroom, or go to my room without instinctively reaching for them. It took five more months, though, before I stopped forcing myself to use the crutches and I started forgetting they were even there.

That doesn't mean walking was easy; just getting up to move around was exhausting. I had lost all of my strength and endurance. I kept telling myself not to give up, to never quit, and my efforts were rewarded with the leg starting to feel and look more normal. I heard about athletes who used electrical stimulation to aid healing and rehabilitation and started to wonder if I could hook my leg up to a car battery or something while I slept. My father actually laughed out loud when I broached that subject, the thought of my leg hooked up to jumper cables adding some much needed levity to the mix.

Because I still had a lot of anger stored up inside me, I started to use it to fuel my efforts to get better. The pain when I moved was dagger-sharp at first, abating so slowly that I barely noticed, until finally I could sleep through the night without it constantly waking me and get up the next morning without surging pain as my wake-up call. My initial goal was to get back to school and, once I'd accomplished that, I continued to push myself to see what my limits were, a tall order for a ten-year-old fifth grader.

With the crutches all but abandoned after another few months, I began to ride my bike and that hurt too. I tried in-line skating, and that was even worse. I started to run but that was the worst of all. Small victories didn't seem to matter so much in the face of so many setbacks and defeats. All told between the braces and my prolonged recovery from surgery, I'd gone more than a year without doing the things I was struggling to do now and, instead of taking solace in the very real progress I was making, I fixated on all that I still couldn't do to the point where it seemed I'd made no progress at all. I still needed the crutches. Not all the time, but enough, which was too much. And some days I felt as if I'd made no progress at all.

Especially when the most painful thing was just sitting down. That simple motion nobody ever thinks twice about forced my hip up against another part of the bone in the hip and socket. It would actually pinch a nerve, sending jabbing stabs of pain through me. I ended up on prescription pain medicine, because the doctors figured less pain meant the freedom of movement to do more.

They tried every drug available at the time to see which might work with a minimum of side effects. The only one that really did was morphine, but being a zombie all the time had me swearing off it; I decided the pain was preferable. I'm not saying I gave up, lost hope, but I was starting to believe that I couldn't do this, that this was my lot in life and I just had to deal with it. You can only overcome so much.

I began to worry about what my future was going to be like and, worse, what my life could've been if this had never happened to me. Nobody realizes how hard it is to be different until they're forced to be. I started to fear that my whole life was going to be like this, limping around like Tiny Tim from Dickens' *A Christmas Carol*, inevitably drawing sympathetic stares from children and adults who were out there living normal lives and walking on their own two feet. One of the truly worst feelings in the world is to look at yourself and hate what you see.

It makes you angry, it makes you sad, and it makes you feel sorry for yourself because you're nothing like you want to be. It's not just your dreams that are dead, it's your hope. You stop being able to see things getting any better, because you honestly don't remember what that felt like. But that's what you're stuck with, and that's what you'll always be stuck with. First chained to my leg braces, then my cast, and finally crutches I'd been warned I might never be able to shed.

I thought about my mother, thought about my father, and I thought about my big brother and my really close friends. I was tired of them feeling sorry for me and having to treat me differently because of my condition. I started thinking: let me make it through today—just today. If I can push through the pain today, maybe I'll be a little bit stronger tomorrow. Living one day at a time kept me from giving up altogether, greeting each morning in the hope I'd feel at least a little bit better, a little bit stronger. Even if it's only one percent.

One day my older brother and my dad found a framed picture of a stork trying to swallow a frog and the frog choking out the bird so it wouldn't get swallowed. For some reason, I saw that as my life in allegory. I was like the frog and the frog had never given up.

That's how he survived and that's the only way I could get better. I remember around that same time hearing the great basketball coach Jimmy Valvano give a speech on ESPN about never giving in to cancer, that you can't let it beat you even if you're losing. That resonated with me so deeply, and I kept seeing Jimmy V in my head even after he died. I wasn't going to lose, nor was I going to let my condition beat me. I was going to put my hands around the neck of life and squeeze back as it tried to swallow me.

But that intention didn't take my pain away. It didn't change the fact that God gave me abilities and then stripped them away. What was I missing here? There must've been a reason, something I was supposed to learn or for which I was being prepared. Living day to day, though, basking in victories no matter how small, kept my focus on the smaller picture instead of the larger one. I wanted to look in the mirror and see someone I liked and was proud of looking back. But every time I looked in the mirror now, all I saw was someone weak and feeble, an inferior version of who I was supposed to be.

I was tired of being a burden, tired of feeling sorry for myself, tired of bemoaning all the things I couldn't do. But one day, as I was staring at myself in the mirror, something changed.

Suddenly I saw myself older and stronger and standing straight. It felt more like a vision than simply conjured from my imagination. I actually believe I'd caught a fleeting glimpse of the Navy SEAL I was destined to become and, even more than that, a man who could be proud of all he'd achieved and all he'd contributed to others. The image lingered in my mind, one of those rare moments in life that was truly a turning point, because that vision had at long last instilled hope in the form of a glimpse of what I could still be.

From that moment on, it was no longer a question of if I was going to get better, but when and how. I put new effort into my thrice-daily exercise routine and redoubled my commitment to the physical therapy sessions my father would drive me to three days a week. Those hour-long sessions had to be moved to five thirty in the morning, because I was finally able to start going to school again.

Have you ever seen the look on a baby's face when he walks for the first time? That's what I felt like the day I put weight on my left leg without using crutches. I didn't get any farther than the baby. I didn't fall, though, and the next day I went a little farther. It still hurt, but even the pain felt different.

Nearly eighteen months from the time my mother had first taken me to the doctor, everything felt different. I still had a long, long way to go, only now I knew I could get there. And I wasn't going to let anything get in my way.

What You Can Learn from This...

1. Being normal is abnormal. At some point in time I needed to be okay with the fact that I was made perfectly imperfect. That through horrible situations, greatness is being forged.

2. Everybody deals with some kind of demon that keeps them from achieving success. Everyone has an excuse for not reaching their goals. Bad things happen to all people, not just me, or you. It is a part of life. You will always be attacked by this demon who prowls around like a lion in the night waiting to devour you. Be ready, be bold, make a choice.

3. Pain lets you know that you are still alive. It lets you know that you have a heart and soul. Unknown to many, pain is actually the source of growth, disguised as something we fear more than anything. Pain, whether caused by others or self-inflicted, should tell you to push past it, move forward, and keep going. No pain, no gain.

CHAPTER 3

Running with Scissors

Lansing, Michigan; 1986

It seems crazy to me that most people cannot remember their childhood. Most people say, "Oh, that was so long ago. I can't even remember last week." I guess my brain is wired differently than most, which seems strange, given there's so much from those years I could have done without, too many casts and crutches. Call it a blessing and a curse I got from my grandmother, who'd regale me with stories about walking to school uphill both ways when she was my age.

I actually remember a great deal from the time I was four years old, like my mother telling me that I wasn't allowed go past the fence on the corner of our street because she couldn't see me if I went past that point. I never did; I always did the right thing, until one day just after I'd turned four. Both my parents were gone and my older brother, Cass, was looking after me at the tender age of ten. We took a walk outside with his friends, and then we got to that dreaded point of no return. I looked at him and he stared back, deep into my eyes, ushering these oft-used words to the point of cliché:

"Don't tell Mom."

And I never did. So, Mom, if you're reading this now, I'm sorry. From the fence line, we proceeded on an adventure to McDonald's, where I got free water, and then we returned home. It wasn't much, but it felt like a lot, because it was the first time I'd had a taste of adventure alone on my own. I felt like Columbus with McDonald's cast as my New World.

Hey, you've got to start somewhere, right?

Before the cast and crutches, I remember climbing the trees in our front yard. I would climb all the way to the top and pretend I was at the peak of the Earth looking out into the world, looking for the next big adventure beyond McDonald's. Later, I realized that those trees were just big bushes; I was so little, they seemed bigger, and my imagination was always more than happy to fill in the blanks. Those big, tall trees might've just been bushes, but I climbed them on my own and wasn't about to stop, even when I got scared. I don't know anybody who really likes heights, but I wasn't about to let that stop me; I wasn't going to let anything stop me from getting to the top.

On a hot summer day in mid-August 1987, on Stafford Avenue, the UPS man came with a huge box. My older brother and his friends were all playing basketball in our backyard. So everyone saw the box and wanted to know what it was.

"I'll open it!" Cass volunteered.

And he did. My dad was still at work and my mother was asleep after working nights, so the responsibility fell to him as the next oldest in the family.

We got the box open, and there it was: an all-red bicycle with a picture of a motorcycle rider on the seat—my dream machine!

"What, you just going to stand there?" Danny and Dequarius, Cass's best friends, who were always around the house with us, said to him in virtual unison. "Well?"

So my brother and his friends assembled my new bike. They did an awesome job too. I remember everybody working together to help "Little Cass," a name I heard my whole life growing up in the gigantic shadow of a great older brother.

Before too long, they had the whole bike assembled and my brother told me to hop on. Of course, they hadn't noticed the training wheels, and had forgotten to screw them on. But who needed training wheels, anyway? Not me. They were for ordinary kids, not one like me who could climb to the highest points of the Earth in my own yard.

"You don't want them?" Cass asked me, holding the training wheels in his hand, having just plucked them from the refuse tucked back into that big box.

"I don't want them."

"Maybe you should. Maybe."

I shook my head adamantly. "No."

If he didn't need them on his bike, I didn't need them on mine. I was Little Cass, after all.

So Big Cass put me on the bike and held me up with his hand, guiding me from the back of the seat. We went around the driveway in a circle for what only seemed to be a couple of minutes, and before I knew it all his friends were cheering me on, and I saw my brother standing beside them with a grin on his face that will never leave my memory.

With the help of my brother I had ridden a bike on the first try without training wheels!

My confidence in myself was so high that nothing could bring me down. By that time both of my parents were there to see what he had done for me, and what I'd accomplished. It just doesn't get any better than that.

Cass was bigger, stronger, faster, and more aggressive than I could even dream of; a meat-eating T. rex of a brother. My first real fight came when I was in second grade, hanging out with this kid named Reese Davis who was in third. This kid named Shane, a real bully who was a year older than Reese and two years older than me, came up from behind Reese and started choking him out for no reason; just because he was bigger and could get away with it, I guess. A real jerk. I didn't know what to do—what *could* I do? I looked at Reese and his face was turning purple, so I said the first thing that popped into my head.

"Hey, pick on someone your own size!"

"Like you?" came Shane's snarling retort.

And he dropped Reese to come after me.

Little did he know that my brother had showed me some of the karate that he'd learned, so I thought I could take him, even though he had three years and a whole bunch of pounds on me. He charged me like a bull, but I was quick on my feet so I sidestepped him just like a matador. By the time he turned around to come at me again, I had already jumped onto his back. His hair was long for a boy's, so I grabbed it to pull myself up to get my arm around his neck, to choke him out the same way he'd tried to choke out Reese. He vigorously tried to fling me off but I had a tight grip and managed to avoid the blows from his flailing fists.

Without thinking I started to punch him in the face with my free hand, several times, to the point where I started to think I was winning. I even hit him hard enough to buckle his knees and knock him down.

Bad idea.

Because now we were both on the ground, with me at a big disadvantage, given the size difference. He tossed me off his back like a rag doll and punched me in the nose. Blood gushed from both nostrils, my eyes tearing up. He kept hitting me and when my vision finally cleared, I spotted a figure tearing toward us on a bike down the hill from where my house was.

It was Cass, pedaling away on his ten-speed bike faster than the Flash himself, so fast his feet churned in a blur, heading straight for me. Before I could register another thought, he'd leaped off the bike and let it clamor to the ground. Then he grabbed the bully Shane and unleashed a blinding flurry of punches that would've made

Bruce Lee proud. All the kids around me in the big crowd that had suddenly gathered were cheering.

Where had they all come from? I wondered, still firmly planted on the ground with my shirt spotted with big globs of blood.

When he was finished with Shane, Cass helped me up and shouted, "Nobody messes with my brother!" back at the bully's squirming form.

Wow! My hero, my own brother!

I looked at him a little differently from that point on. I never forgot what his coming to my rescue meant to me, how important it was to have the back of someone important to you. That and learning to ride a bike without training wheels are things that left an indelible impression that still sticks with me today. Thinking back now, I wonder in wanting to become a Navy SEAL, a hero for others, if I was really trying to become Cass.

I looked up to him, not just physically either. It seemed to me that everything he did was far better than anything that I could ever do, and that was just something that came naturally for him. Part of his yoke. He was tough on me, because he was my brother, and he never wanted me to be taken advantage of. He knew he wouldn't always be there to save me and wanted me to be able to save myself. In my mind that made him the perfect brother. He took me places where I wasn't supposed to go, took care of me and watched over me. When we did things together, I thought it was gold.

He was amazing at sports too, far better than I could ever hope to be. Basketball was our sport and he was exceptional, his jump shot seeming to go in every time he fired the ball up. And he had this uncanny ability to jump over things and people, a vertical leap you wouldn't believe. I remember how he put a mix tape together when he was in high school of him just dunking the ball for hours. Speaking of which, when it came to music, he could play pretty much any instrument. Guitar, bass, piano, drums—you name it and he could play it, and play it flawlessly. Everything seemed natural for him, seemed to come easy. Whatever he did, like music, just flowed out of him.

And it wasn't as if he had a lot of time to practice or took lessons or anything. He'd hear the song, hear the chords. Then play the chords, adjust the chords, and make it a cooler song. Meanwhile, it took me months before I could play even the C and C minor on the guitar, before I gave up on the effort. There was nothing Cass couldn't do or make look easier than it should've been. I know it's natural to look up to and want to emulate an older brother like Cass. But I always saw him more like a picture in a sports magazine, or a character from television, as someone I could never be.

That's a hard thing for a kid and it became a burden for me, because I couldn't do anything as well or as easily as Cass could. So how was I supposed to make my mom and dad proud the way he did? How could I make them notice me? In retrospect, I guess it was more about noticing myself. You know, self-esteem.

But I wasn't going to give up. I kept trying, even though the results weren't there the way they'd been for Cass, in sports or anything else. It was so hard accepting the fact that I was never going to measure up to my older brother. It was like trying to scale a flat wall that had nothing to hold onto. The picture I painted in my head of who I wanted to be was him, but I never had enough brushes or even paint to make that happen.

Like the time he let me appear on stage with him.

Fast-forward to after I'd graduated high school and was about to enlist in the Navy. Cass had put together a band with some friends. They'd played shows regularly and even appeared on local radio. Then came the night he let me come on stage with him to join in a kind of duet with me singing backup vocals. What an opportunity to prove myself, not only to him, but to the world, and myself, that I could be like him. Even though the gap in our ages seemed so much smaller than it had when he taught me how to ride a bike, that moment made me feel like a little boy again with something big to prove.

It didn't go nearly as well as that first bike ride around the driveway.

I started in before I was supposed to, destroying the entire band's rhythm. He flashed me a look that stretched well beyond dissatisfaction, even approaching disgust. His eyes lit up so all I could see were the whites and he shook his head to signal me to stop. I could tell that he was not just pissed off, but disappointed at the same time. He knew something like that was probably going to happen. I'd let him down, and I'd let myself down. Boy, did that hurt. I don't think I've ever felt smaller or more insignificant.

I don't know what had even led him to let me go on stage with his band; maybe it was because I spent so much time listening to them practice, or maybe he just wanted to give me a chance, to make me feel good. After all, how bad could it be?

Pretty bad, as things turned out.

After that day, years after I'd shed the leg braces and crutches, I decided to make a list of the things that I could do, even if I couldn't excel at them, and resolved to stop judging myself so harshly. Even more, I promised to stop measuring myself up to Cass, because that was an impossible bar I could in no way meet, especially given that he was almost six years older than me. I couldn't be him and I'd been foolish, as all kids are when it comes to such things, to believe that I could. I remembered an old saying that says to beware of your idols, since they may disappoint you. That saying makes no mention of what it feels like when the reverse is true.

That said, my brother, unwittingly or otherwise, had motivated me to accept nothing less than the highest possible standards for myself, by pushing me to my absolute limits. I remember when I finally, at long last, beat him in a game of one-on-one basketball. I was fifteen at the time and felt like a king. It was like life had just tilted off its axis. Because if I could be that good in one thing, I could be that good in all, or at least many, things. Maybe he let me win; it doesn't matter because he made me work hard and, in that sense, that ethos had already made me a winner.

Not long after I rode that gleaming new bike around the driveway, my family moved. The new place was clearly an upgrade from our two-bedroom, 700-square-foot home, to a house that had three bedrooms and a full basement. When the same friends from whom I was moving came to visit, we'd have a great place to play.

The last night before the move, I remember telling the house, as if it were alive, that it was great and I'd always miss it. I slept only on my little mattress that night, the bedcovers all packed away. The sadness didn't dissipate until we rolled into the driveway of our new home, so much bigger, with a great yard and everything. As we were unloading our 1984 blue Ford pickup truck, I noticed all these girls staring out the window in the house across the street. One, two, three, four girls looking out the window! They were probably checking out my handsome brother, Cass. He was tall, tan, brown-eyed, and strong. Who wouldn't check him out? If Brad Pitt had been there, I'm sure the girls would've checked him out too.

Just as it was love at first sight for those schoolgirls with Cass, so it was with us as soon as we laid eyes on our new home. We ran inside, no less giddy than the girls across the street had been upon ogling Cass. We played hide-and-seek, we claimed our rooms, and helped Mom and Dad move in. I took a look at the backyard and fell even more in love. It was a boy's dream, with pine trees so tall you could climb higher than the house, and there were the woods, real woods, at the back of the lot. That sight immediately conjured up visions in my head of playing GI Joe and building a fort, going exploring. The possibilities were endless compared to where we'd come from.

Yup, I was coming up in the world, literally when you compare the bushes I used to climb to those big pine trees.

To top it all off, I met Whitney, who was going into kindergarten, just like me. She told me that, "David lives next door and we're best friends. We're the same age, but I'm older by one day." I met David, and the three of us fast became the best of friends, to the point where everyone called us the three amigos!

I was a little older, so I would always try to do something over the top, something they never thought of or had seen before. I wasn't trying to impress them; I was more or less thinking of new ways to make any stunt more exciting or adventurous, and sometimes even dangerous. I was always the first to do something, then David, and then eventually, after I'd do it a few more times, Whitney would build up the courage to try it too. She did things that no other girl in the neighborhood ever do; I guess I was rubbing off on her—in a good way, just like my brother had rubbed off on me.

David was always busy finding out what scheme he could pull off to get me to do something crazy. I always knew what his plans were, and they were always a challenge. Knowing me, though, he knew I'd never back down from a challenge or gave up just because I didn't succeed the first time. I loved the fact that David would push me to the point I had never been to. He'd do it every day, and I'd accept the challenge every time.

I guess the legacy Cass had left me with was a desire to perform the impossible and to be disappointed when I failed to achieve it. One day, while climbing a tree next to Whitney's house, I decided to go from the tree to the roof. I got the idea and didn't hesitate; I just did it, swinging off the tree and landing on the roof, and there I was on top of a house looking down at my two friends, who must've felt the same way I did when I looked up to Cass, figuratively and literally. Eventually David and Whitney followed my path up, just like I'd followed my brother up on stage years later, only they didn't disappoint me the way I'd disappointed him.

There was another time the woodpile behind the garage grew high enough to reach a ledge from which you could climb onto the roof of the garage, so I did that too, but the real cool thing that I had in mind was to jump off the roof and do a tuck and roll once I hit the ground.

"No way!" said David. "You can't do that! No way."

"That's crazy!" Whitney added. "You'll kill yourself. You're only seven years old."

Well, I'll show them, I thought, intent on delivering the goods I hadn't when trying to emulate Cass. I took the leap.

Now, understand that I couldn't just drop off the edge of the roof, because there were bushes that extended out past the edge by four feet, so I had to make sure that leap took me a good distance out to clear the shrubs. In those brief moments, I felt like I was an eagle flying high in the sky, one of those moments where time stops and then picks up again in slow motion.

What a great feeling. I landed just as I wanted to, then rolled out of the landing exactly like a Ninja would. David and Whitney looked at me with disbelief when I stood up. But I just smiled and said, "Who's coming with me to do it again?"

I got David to follow, after I taught him how to land starting off a smaller ledge. It took him about five minutes but he did it, and he was proud and glad I coaxed him into trying. Whitney got on the roof but kept her feet firmly planted upon it, until about a week later when she swallowed her fear and took the plunge. She did it, but she never did it again. Once was enough for Whitney.

On Saturday mornings, just David and I would go and practice shooting the bow and arrow. One Saturday morning, we got tired of picking pinecones off the tree out back and decided to up the ante a bit by seeing how far we could shoot the arrow and stay accurate. Like any two normal boys, we kept trying to outdo each other. We both thought it would be a good idea to see who could shoot the arrow into the backyard fence. I drew the bow back, felt the tension on all of my muscles as I aimed it as high as I thought was needed to achieve the best possible angle, and released the arrow.

It flew so high we thought it had touched the clouds. But then...

"Uh-oh," David said.

My sense of pride in the shot all washed away when I noticed the angle was going to carry the arrow over the fence instead. It came down with such force and speed, like a rocket zooming in on a target, and then *whack*! The arrow had lodged right into the roof of the backyard neighbor's house. And not just any neighbor either:

Old Man Peabody!

Even now, that name strikes fear in me.

David and I ran inside and huddled next to a window of his room that looked out over Old Man Peabody's yard to see what might happen next, practically holding our breath.

Who could blame us? Old Man Peabody hated kids, and we'd just stuck an arrow into his house. How were we going to get the thing out, without him catching us trespassing on his property? Man, he'd probably cook us with the rabbits that he ate since, in his mind, we were no better than they were.

We ate some lunch and discussed a plan to remove the arrow. David was going to go around my backyard to the big willow tree, climb it, and look down toward Old Man Peabody's yard—an early warning system for me—while I climbed the fence and scaled that side of his house. We had our calls ready and made sure to communicate, so that we would achieve mission success. Even though my hip hurt, in an eerie precursor to the experience I'd face later, I knew that I could do it. So long as I could jump from the gas meter to the pipe on the side to the window, I could jump from the window ledge and then to the gutter. From there, all I had to do was shimmy up to the roof and, from that point, it would be easy as cake.

As I approached the house and climbed onto the gas meter, David gave me the all-clear call with a crow sound.

"Cawwwwwwwwwww!"

Talk about successful mission parameters! I jumped to the gas meter and with my one good leg leaped to the pipe on the side. The leap felt as if it took a whole minute, and then, *bam*, I grabbed hold of the pipe with my left arm stretched to its limits, and then added my right for good measure. I reached for the window ledge, my arms spread out as far as they could go. I was slipping and got a little scared, but there was no way that I was going back to the ground, not without that arrow. I swung from the pipe to the window ledge and made it, but my feet hit the side of the house before I could swing them up and over it.

Just as I got up to the ledge, Old Man Peabody came to the window and looked outside.

My fingers were, literally, right underneath his eyes and I heard him grumbling under his breath. My heart was beating out of my chest, and I thought for sure he saw my fingers, as I hung on for dear life. The moment I thought he was going to open the window and look down straight at me, he abruptly turned around and disappeared from sight. After a few seconds, I pulled myself up to check the room.

The window was foggy, so I couldn't really see inside. I figured if I couldn't see him, even he was still in the room somewhere, he couldn't see me either. So I climbed into the crevasse of the windowsill and got ready to leap to the gutter and the roof.

Just as I started a mental count to three in my head, I heard David screech the warning signal:

"Cawwwwwww! Cawwwwwwww!"

Someone was coming, and I had no place to go. Nothing I could do but get caught scaling a neighbor's house. I made eye contact with David across the way and he pointed downward. I didn't see exactly at what initially, but he kept at it, jabbing the air until it looked like he was pointing right at me. I turned my gaze downward and saw none other than Old Man Peabody walk underneath me. He looked out to the fence and started swearing under his breath. He picked up an old tennis ball that one of the kids threw over the fence, pulled out a knife that looked like it came from a slasher film, and stabbed the tennis ball. Then he threw it back over the fence and continued around the house, passing right beneath me en route to his backyard.

It was now or never. I leaped to the gutter, pulled myself up, and crawled like Spiderman to reach the arrow. I glanced to the weeping willow tree, toward David.

"*Caw*," he said softer, signaling the coast was clear.

I yanked the arrow out and threw it back into my yard like a javelin thrower in the Olympics. After that I just lay down flat on the roof to steady my nerves, calm myself. Just then, I heard the garage open and saw Old Man Peabody's old car pull out of the driveway. Afraid I might be in his line of sight, I leaped to the other side of the roof and peered over the top to watch the old man backing up and then turning onto the street. But I still didn't move, not until his car was out of sight at last. I saw David hop out of the tree like a monkey, looking up at me now from the ground.

"I thought you were dead meat," he said, grinning.

I moved to the edge of the roof, jumped off, and landed by doing my patented tuck and roll. I popped up and we walked away laughing, promising myself I'd never do anything like that again, a promise that didn't last too long.

I believe to this day that my relationship with Cass superheated my already competitive nature. I never looked for the easy way to do something; I looked for the way in which I could come out ahead of everyone else. That included a challenge I laid out for David and Whitney: I told them I was going to beat them home from school, even though we got out at the same time and they always got a ride from David's mom, Nora, who worked at the school. I'd bolt out of school as soon as the bell rang and run home along the fastest route I could find, while David and Whit had to wait for their ride. That gave me a five-minute head start I took full advantage of.

I'd always see David's mom before I left the school, because her office was right by the main door that I took to leave.

"Do you want a ride?" she'd ask me practically every day, not realizing she was my competition.

"No, thank you," I'd always reply politely, and then burst through the doors and run full speed straight to my house.

I lived about a mile from the school, but a little less as the crow flies. I would run down the big hill and cut every corner I could to try and beat my two best friends back home. I would slide through the first fence between where the bushes met the fence at Mr. Maurice's house and cut through his front yard to the other street. After the first shortcut I would then streamline through the woods, but I had to cut through Old Man Peabody's yard, of all places, to do so. Not surprisingly, this was the hardest part of the trek. Any day could be the day he'd be lying in wait for me, and I'd disappear forever.

"Don't you cut through my yard! I'm calling the cops!" he'd rage every time he spotted me, but he never did lay in wait or catch up with me, when he gave chase.

After making it through his and other backyards, I'd be on the edge of the woods. Moving at a full sprint, from there I only had one more fence to hop to beat David and Whitney home. The final yard I used as a bypass belonged to my crush, Heather McNealy. I loved coming over to use her trampoline, which gave me an excuse to see Heather, even though she was four years older. Young love— what can I say? Unlike Old Man Peabody, I always hoped she was watching for me.

I'd run up the wooden stairs from her backyard back onto the street, which put me three houses away from a right turn onto my street. I knew that if I was on my street and Nora's car was still anywhere behind me, I'd win. During the sprint from the woods through the backyards there would be openings to the streets, so I could spot Nora's car on the road and, based on where it was, could gauge how fast I needed to run when turns and stop signs were figured into the mix. After I got home, I'd run into my room and change my shirt and go back outside, as if I'd been waiting there all day for them to catch up to me.

Before the cast and crutches came, this kind of friendly competition came to define my life, what I enjoyed most. Riding our bikes in "the Pit," an old gravel quarry, especially was a blast. The Pit featured some seriously fun jumps and old dirt paths laid out like a natural track; it felt like an adventure every single time we rode there. There was also this old legend that a black bear lived in the hole underneath Stacey Kipers' backyard right next door. So, of course I had to check it out. Another of my friends, Ryan Fitzpatrick, was so scared he was almost crying by the time we were down ten feet. I told him to wait back up at the opening. And, hey, it was scary in there; cold, wet, and dark. As it turned out, it was just a water runoff that ran underground.

I remember keeping up with this kid Lamar in a race, when I was in third grade and he was the fastest fifth grader. He beat me, but I knew that someday I'd get my rematch, and I worked toward that every day in the Pit to build my confidence and make sure I was ready when the time came. Before I got my rematch with Lamar, I challenged an eighteen-year-old named Brian to a race. I thought for sure I could beat him, and David thought so too. David's dad even made a bet with him. Brian was in shape and played tennis so, yes, he did beat me, but not by much. So I placed yet another rematch on my bucket list.

Speed was my friend, my ally. Being fast can get you out of many things, but because it couldn't get me out of everything, I followed my older brother into the study of karate. Before long, I took first place in my division as a fighter among a bunch of kids who were ranked higher than I was. Some of them were bigger too. Pu kung tang was the actual style I was studying, and the art was great for building mental toughness that allowed students to withstand and overcome whatever's thrown at them, without losing their temper or confidence. I loved to fight, to test my skills as a fighter; there was just nothing else like it, in large part because there was no ceiling on your abilities, no limits other than the ones you imposed on yourself.

Karate became a huge staple in my life. For self-defense, for discipline, for any number of things. I was very fortunate that my instructor, my sensei, was an old-school, traditional kind of guy. First thing you did when you entered the dojo was take off your shoes. And there was absolutely no goofing off, joking around, or saying anything even remotely out of line. At first, you'd go home with your knuckles bloodied, your body bruised, and blisters all over your feet. My sensei made us work for everything. Nothing came easy and, looking back on it, it was kind of like SEAL training for a kid. My sensei wasn't about to keep promoting students just because they kept showing up. He was all about being able to put the techniques he taught us into practice, both in competition and in self-defense, should we ever need to. He wanted us to be prepared and he wanted us to be capable of defending ourselves in real-world situations, so we wouldn't panic when we found ourselves in a hostile environment or situation.

We endured intense training hours, focused on hard work and discipline, when we trained at the dojo. I learned how to punch, how to kick, how to block, how to sweep, how to move, to sidestep. I learned how to disarm someone with a knife or a gun, and I continued to hone my skills in hand-to-hand combat. And I wasn't the only one in the family to do so either; my father was in the class, along, of course, with my brother Cass. I was the youngest student when I finally got started, and there were times where I got knocked down face-first. My sensei wanted me to be strong and instilled in me the belief that discipline and the right mindset could overcome any and all odds. In fact, a sign posted over the door said it all:

CAN'T IS NOT IN MY VOCABULARY

Words to live by, at the dojo and beyond it. And right next to the sign was a photo of a man with all of the pressure points you could use to take somebody out and escape a hostile situation. Studying karate was vital to me in other ways beyond the physical. It taught me that small, incremental steps of pain and struggle are required to get where you want to go, to achieve your goals literally then, but also figuratively as the years went on. Success doesn't just come because you wanted it. Being the best, or excelling, at anything is all about discipline, dedication, and hard work.

I went to tournaments all around the state and fought against others from other styles, ranks, and abilities. I never cared about, or let myself be intimidated by size or rank when I faced the opponent across from me. And I won more than my share of bouts because I never backed down from an opponent. Once I was in the zone, nothing else mattered.

Until something, suddenly, did.

In two years of studying karate, I felt like nothing could stop me, but one day that all changed. The inside of my leg started hurting and I thought that I'd just pulled a groin muscle. The doctor suggested ibuprofen and a warm bath. Ice it down after karate and you'll be fine, he told me.

But after a month I wasn't. I was having difficulty sleeping and my mom noticed that I was complaining for the first time in my life about a physical pain. She knew something was wrong and I guess I did too, though I didn't want to admit it.

We had taken a trip to Disney World with relatives who lived in Florida and my mom noticed that when I ran with my older brother, something didn't look right, because I was favoring my good leg so much. That's when she made the decision that we were going to see a specialist once we got home.

And, not too long after that, I was on the road to the longest year of my life.

What You Can Learn from This...

1. Being a kid and having a positive environment can change your thinking and give you the building blocks of friendships that last a lifetime. I know I would not be the same person I am today if I didn't have that connection with those who I love, trust, and go to in times of trouble.

2. Your circumstances will be bad, but don't let bad things or circumstances dictate who you are or what you could become.

3. Dare to dream about what could happen when you're young.

CHAPTER 4

Back On My Three Feet

Lansing, Michigan, 1993

Sometimes you have to do what your body says you can't. Sometimes you have to take ownership of what's wrong with you, as opposed to letting it own you. That's the way it was for me.

I was finally cleared to return to school, even though I wasn't cleared to do much of anything else. My brother was a senior in high school at the time and I got my confidence back by following him around on my crutches and leg braces, trying to keep up with him as he was warming up before playing basketball games on the varsity team. He would intentionally slow down when he was next to me, just so I'd be able to keep up with him; he didn't have to but he did.

My mother was sitting in the stands with my father, watching all this, every time my brother would warm up during the season. Once, she overheard the woman seated next to her say something that made her skin crawl:

"I feel so sorry for that crippled boy."

"He's not crippled," my mother snapped at her. "It's a bone disease, all right? A bone disease. Oh, and by the way, he's my son."

Sure, everyone in my family felt sorry for me and they were mad that something like this could happen to someone they loved. But they were also scared, because they didn't really know what the future held and neither did I. I was afraid my life would never be the same and no one could offer any assurances otherwise. Not the doctors, not my parents—nobody. The only person who could take charge of my future was me. Was I going to sit or lie around and wait to maybe get better, or was I going to push forward and test my limits? And that's why I resolved to get out of the house and back into the world, specifically back to school, even if I had to crutch myself around.

My days at school were long and hard. People, kids and adults, were always looking at me as if I were a leper, calling me a cripple, just like that woman seated next to my mother, under their breath.

"Run, Forrest, run!" I'd hear them joke, having no idea at the time how prophetic that quip turned out to be.

They called me Squeaky, because the braces on my legs would squeak when my legs would move back and forth. I'd endured painful rehab, a thousand questions, and long nights of crying myself to sleep in silent tears. I went to school with a chip on my shoulder, a thicker skin, and would block out anyone's voice who put me down or made fun of me. That brought on a lot of emotional turmoil and lack of confidence I'd never experienced before. For the first time in my life I was unsure of my abilities and saw the real possibility of not being able to be myself ever again. I fought for every inch of movement in my left leg. I rehabbed, iced, stretched for hours and hours on end, waking up early before school to go to rehab off of Michigan Avenue at 5:30 a.m., but all that seemed not to matter.

My hip refused to get better and I began to face the fact that this might well be a permanent condition. Living with crutches and leg braces, stuck in a position that made me look like I'd just got off a horse. It seemed hopeless. What was I supposed to do? Who was I supposed to talk to who could relate to my problems? I prayed to God, because that was all I could do and maybe He would listen when no one else had.

I'd crutch around the school slowly at first, falling over frequently and having my friends carry my books to class for me. After being on crutches for twelve months, I had plenty of scars and calluses to show for my efforts that left me significantly better able to navigate the world with them. I got fast on the crutches that I learned how to negotiate stairs and corners without missing a step. I tried to treat them as extra appendages, as much a part of me as my other limbs.

Because they were.

Getting better crutching around gave me hope, renewed my confidence, and made me think if I could do this, I could do anything—including get better to the point that someday I'd no longer need them. I started to look at crutching around the same way I did when I rode my first bike without training wheels, or climbed the tree next to Old Man Peabody's house. And I got to be so fast that I could beat some people running. I remember a time leading up to our school's field day when all the students were asked to sign up for the races they wanted to enter. Each teacher had a sign-up sheet, and my choices were limited to the beanbag throw (which I knew I couldn't win because Matt Prebbie had a cannon for an arm) and the three-legged race, after I was told my crutches disqualified me from the fifty-yard dash. Did they think they gave me an unfair advantage or something? Go figure.

The principal knew who I was and called me into her office over the intercom. She had seen that I had put my name under the three-legged race. She asked me how I could do this with a partner when I was on crutches.

"Doctor Turpin," I told her, "I have one good leg and two crutches, that makes three legs. It is the three-legged race, right?"

She smiled at me and said, "Well, yes, it is, but be careful!"

I crushed that race by fifty feet. Nobody could catch me! This was a watershed moment, at least mentally and spiritually. Call it a major breakthrough that really helped me feel better about myself, against a backdrop of so many setbacks and false hopes. I had tried to be a happy little kid, tried to be the same, but it just didn't ever seem to get better, only worse. The pain and suffering, the sleepless nights. I thought all these things were going to bring me to my end, but God had other ideas, starting with the day I won that three-legged race.

I thought after some time passed, people would begin to see me for me, and look past the metal legs with plastic and Velcro wrapped around my thighs. My close friends did do that, but the people who didn't know me, or people that I didn't see regularly, would make comments and snide remarks as I'd pass them in the halls. To a little kid these things hurt deep down to the core, and you don't even know it at the time because things are always new, and you haven't yet got a taste of the real world. While I was confined to the metal and crutches though, I felt like I got more than just a taste—my eyes were opened to how the world truly is. It sucks, people are only out for themselves, and they don't care who they hurt, just as long as they can feel good, or at least better than you, along the way.

I would hear, "What's wrong with your legs? Did your parents beat you?"

Or, "Ride 'em, cowboy. Where's your horse?"

And how about, "Shhhh, here comes the retard," after which they'd always talk very slow and loud to me.

"Hey, it's the Tin Man! Squeak, squeak! Hey Squeaky, come here."

This was a form of bullying that wasn't labeled as such at the time. Things were different back then, I guess, and I just had to deal with the emotional pain and struggle in whatever form of ridicule or finger pointing that came my way. It's almost impossible to stay positive and point yourself in the right direction when everything else is pointing the other way. Everyone, including your parents, is telling you that you can't do the things you once dreamt of doing. The life of a kid is about two things: enjoying today and imagining tomorrow. Well, for me both of those had been taken away.

Most days I could laugh along with the name callers, but there were plenty of days when I couldn't. I learned the hard way that not everyone was kindhearted. People, especially kids, see something different and seem to like the fact it makes them feel superior. I guess it's the natural order of things. They might've felt bad for me but, mostly, they felt good about themselves.

Sometimes people would come up to me and say, "What's wrong with you?" A legitimate question, right? Well, it gets redundant and you just want to wear a sign that explains everything. You want to tell everyone who stares at you, "I'm perfectly fine. I'm normal. You don't have to talk to me like I am deaf or stupid."

You can hear the pity streaming from their voices, but not necessarily from their hearts. As a kid, the only way I could endure this was to build my wall up higher and higher. I guess maybe I thought if it got high enough, they wouldn't be able to see me. A more accurate depiction of those times, though, was that I didn't want to see them and the way they looked at me.

Did they think I wanted the crutches? Didn't they know I wanted to walk like I used to? It didn't seem to matter what anyone thought or knew. They made me feel so small, it was almost like I didn't exist, and maybe I didn't want to exist. The experience wasn't making me tough; it was eating me up inside. The only thing that really kept me going was the drive inside me to be the best no matter what I did— that was no less true at that point than any other. It was just harder to believe in the possibility of being the best at anything.

And things were about to get worse.

Originally, when the crutches and leg braces failed to produce the results doctors had hoped for, there were no other options other than surgery which left me in a body cast for weeks that stretched into months. And after those months came six more with the crutches again.

I think you can see where I'm going with this, so we don't need to belabor the experience any further. Suffice it to say that I ended up going three years without using my left leg at all. So even when the second surgery was pronounced successful as such things go, I was in a lot of pain, excruciating pain trying to get my leg to do the most normal things again. Imagine just walking from the couch into the kitchen as a laborious challenge, and you'll have an idea of what I'm talking about.

Even worse, doctors told me the best I could hope for was to be able to manage tasks like that, and not much more. I could forget about running. I could forget about playing sports. I could forget all about the things I enjoyed the most and had endured so much pain and heartache to be able to do again. How was I supposed to be like my big brother when I couldn't jump off a basketball floor, or chase him down in a foot race? Who was I ever going to be able to save from bullies the way he'd saved me?

Sure, the day finally came when the test results revealed sufficient improvement to finally shed the crutches for good. But the general prognosis was that, if I worked very hard, I could get back to about 60 percent of where I'd been. I didn't care what they said; I was done listening to their pronouncements and predictions. I was determined to prove them all wrong. But they were right about one thing they told me: trying to manage even the simplest tasks hurt; man, did it hurt! I never let on to anyone, my parents and brother included, how much. Because I had a plan.

I didn't just want to be as fast as I'd been before; I wanted to be faster. I ran and I ran and I ran some more. I ran home from Pattengill Middle School to my house, about five miles every day. I'd run two miles home from basketball practice near my old elementary school every Tuesday and Thursday evening, even in the snow. I kept running and kept getting stronger, even though the pain was getting worse. So I'd run home, only to lay in the bathtub, on my bed, or on the couch. I couldn't sit down normally because of the angle of my leg and my hip in the socket. If I went to sit down, my leg would lock into position and it felt like daggers were jabbing away deep inside my hip socket. If I rotated my leg in the slightest way, it would pinch the nerve and send shooting pain from the back of my neck down to the tips of my toes. I couldn't internally or externally rotate my hip socket. I couldn't squat to even seventy degrees. My range of motion was more than limited. It was a painful grinding, popping, and clicking experience just to sit down at the lunch table in the cafeteria. Everything was a struggle.

My good friend David (remember him from the Old Man Peabody adventure?) moved away to Okemos, which was about eight miles from my house. After school got out on Friday, I would ride my bike all the way over there to hang out with him. Most of the time I would stay the night and ride back home the next day. Biking felt easier on my leg than running, and even sitting on the bicycle seat felt better than a chair or couch because I didn't have to sit down on the bike seat at all! I realized that if I kind of stood up and pedalled, then my leg didn't hurt too much at all, so that was one of the biggest reliefs in my life up to that point. I'd ride my bike all over town. As long as my parents knew where I was headed, they were okay with me heading out on my own. The relative ease with which I biked made me think that maybe I'd focused too much on running as both a means and an end. Maybe there were even more activities that would be easier on my hip and would help me get stronger on top of that.

So I tried in-line skating from my house to David's house and back again, sometimes all in one day. I wasn't just coping anymore; I was actually getting better, I thought, at least enough to give me the motivation I needed to keep pressing on. My muscles were strong and getting stronger each time I made the journey. Real progress! Except the bone at the hip socket was still causing me excruciating pain. I was dealing with the pain better, but it was still there and showed no signs of abating. The whole thing became a classic zero-sum game: I wanted to hang out with David, more than I hated the pain I had to endure to get to his house. I couldn't let the pain get in the way, and even if I couldn't get rid of it, I wasn't going to let it control my life. Before I was angry at the world. Now I turned my anger more inward; I was angry at the pain, and I wasn't going to let it beat me. I would just bottle it deep down inside and use that as a source of power when I needed it most or wanted to cry.

School was the worst. It hurt so bad to try and sit in the chairs during class, because my hip would not move into the seated position that everyone else is so accustomed to using. The most comfortable position for the rest of the world was the most painful for me. I would get in trouble for slouching, or getting up too many times in class. Teachers didn't like me disrupting their classes, in spite of the fact pain was forcing me to. And I was just trying to ease the pain so I wouldn't cry. Whitney had followed David to a different school, so I no longer had anyone to confide in, who I knew had my back. I remember when I was housebound how desperately I wanted to get back to school. Now I'd wake up in the morning, dreading the day that was to come.

My mom and dad would ask me on a daily basis if I was okay, if I wanted to talk or if there was anything they could do.

"No, it's okay. I'm fine."

I didn't want them to worry about me. They'd already lost one son, my brother Cameron, to leukemia, something I don't talk about a lot and not very well at all when I do. I didn't like the notion of being a burden, sparking the kind of memories that would bring back the tragedy they'd never moved on from, but at least had come to accept. The last thing I wanted was to steal smiles from their faces and replace them with long, drawn looks and frowns. I didn't want to make them sad, I wanted to make them proud. And my brother's death provided an odd kind of motivation in the sense that it wasn't just for me that I desperately wanted to get better; it was for my parents and older brother Cass too. To spare them from feeling the kind of pain on the inside I was feeling on the outside. It became a kind of moral responsibility for me, the least I could do after all the time, effort, and money they spent nursing me back to a level of health that had already exceeded the doctors' predictions. So, as far as they knew, I was never in pain, or the pain that I experienced was easily manageable, kind of like ordinary aches. If they didn't have to worry about me, I wouldn't have to worry about them worrying about me, if that makes any sense.

"Don't worry, I'm fine."

That's what I always said as I shrugged off their desire to reach out to me. I guess I wasn't too good at fooling them. They must've known how hard things continued to be and, in that respect, probably felt as helpless as I did. But they didn't want to push things too far on that note, because there was nothing to be gained from it, other than to make me feel even worse. I had built that wall so high and so thick nobody was going to get through it to me. I was tired of people feeling sorry for me and thinking I was different. Better to put up barriers than to have my life riddled by the insecurity that came whenever I let them down.

Some days, I'd be walking down the hallway and someone would bump or nudge into me intentionally, more than enough for my leg to lock up, pinch my nerves, and make me fall over and drop my books or backpack or anything that was in my hands. I'd lose control of the feeling in my extremities because of the pain that ensued. And the pain remained just as bad when I was sitting down. Sometimes it felt someone had stabbed me and was grinding the knife into my hipbone.

Visits to Doctor Hensinger were always the same. I was in his office for the second time in three months in Ann Arbor at the University of Michigan orthopedic department. This hospital is one of the best in the United States for my condition and Doctor Hensinger remained tops in his field. Once again, he told me that I couldn't play sports, and that my days as even a recreational athlete were over at the ripe old age of eleven. No matter how much we talked about the pain that had become a staple in my life, his advice was always the same: stop doing anything even remotely physical in nature. It hurt so much to sit, Doctor Hensinger explained, because I was taxing the area by doing too much, which, by my former standards, was hardly anything at all. It hurt so much because the hipbone that deteriorated was now growing back, but in a deformed way.

It was growing way too wide and oblong and jagged. The shape that should resemble a smooth ball and socket with no flaws now looked like a jagged mushed bone and half of a socket. Like someone took a sledgehammer to the joint and hit it as hard as they could. It was flat instead of round. It was bumpy all around where it should have been smooth. The top of the femoral head hardly fit into the also misshapen socket, or top of the hip where it connects to the pelvis.

That was a watershed moment for me, because I had a choice to make. Do I call it quits on trying to become a normal kid again, or do I keep trying to prove pretty much everyone wrong? Around this time, I hung the picture of the stork with a frog stuck in its mouth on my wall. The picture featured the words I intended to live by for as long as it took, even if it was forever:

DON'T QUIT, DON'T EVER QUIT.

Time passed; days into weeks, weeks into months, months into years. Nothing much changed. I wasn't getting any better by the time I reached high school and I wasn't getting any worse. I was in a kind of physical limbo. A good day was one where I managed to avoid the usual modicum of pain, a bad day when my hip kept barking after the simplest of movements or activities. The worst was when I pushed myself to do more, only to be faced with the fact that I could push all I wanted, but the more wasn't coming.

Every time I felt like crying, I bottled it up and used rage to fuel me instead. Maybe that was because of my older brother, who'd tell me repeatedly that, "Boys don't cry; only girls do."

Cass became my driving force for my obsession to be normal again, because I'd watch all the things he did brilliantly and wish I could do them without pain. My brother was a high school star, able to do things that I could only dream about. Even before my condition flared up, I placed Cass on a pedestal that I endeavored to reach no matter how tortuous the climb, because then my parents would look and cheer for me the same way they did for him. Their frustration and heartache was every bit the equal of my own, exacerbated by the financial hole I'd dug for them with all the accumulated medical bills dealing with my condition.

Older now, the onset of puberty having raised my voice without lowering my hopes, I'd tell myself to stop being such a wussy and just ignore the pain. I'd watch movies, highlighted by diatribes like, "Pain is weakness leaving the body," or, "Pain is only temporary." In my case, of course, it was constant. I started reading about the career of Bo Jackson, who'd managed to return to professional baseball with an artificial hip after suffering from an almost identical condition to mine. If he could get his life and dreams back in order, then so could I.

My life, meanwhile, became dominated by proving people wrong and little more. Against my doctor's wishes, I continued to run, to train, then practically inhale ibuprofen when I got home and slather Icy Hot on my leg while putting a heating pad as close to my throbbing hip as possible. All I could do was try to break my condition before it broke me, as it had tried so often over these years that felt like a lifetime.

I turned to basketball as my go-to sport, my personal proving ground to show I could compete with my brother. Cass had a t-shirt that read, "Basketball is life, the rest is just details." He embodied that kind of spirit and perseverance, out every day shooting and doing drills with the hoop in our driveway my dad had to replace something like seventeen times because of repeated damage due to dunking. While growing up, I never had as much interest in organized sports as martial arts; I wanted to be GI Joe or a ninja, not a professional athlete.

Playing basketball, though, offered relief from all the rigors I'd endured and afforded me the opportunity to spend time with my brother. The driveway hoop became a sanctuary. No matter how much pain I was in, I could still hoist up a shot. Once I got off the crutches, in middle school, I joined a junior pro league and our team made it to nationals that took us all the way to Tennessee. At this stage of my life, I wanted and needed to win at something, as opposed to being told I couldn't do this, that, or be what I wanted to be. If I could excel at basketball, then all the pain I had to do endure would be worth it. I needed that competition to get me through the moments where I still felt weak and insignificant.

Basketball became my barometer to prove to myself how far I'd come, that all the work I'd done at rehab was indeed worth something. Playing kept me grounded and in touch with my physical abilities that would, hopefully, continue to improve. If I could run faster than people for the ninety-four foot length of the court, if I could out-jump someone, I was proving I was just as good as everyone else, to others and to myself. Basketball became a measuring stick for me, a different kind of crutch for me to lean on.

One Friday morning I was listening to a guest speaker at our school named Jeremy Kingsley. He acted out a skit where he was a young boy at school putting on different faces to different people. Each time he met someone else he would apply a new face to his mask, and everyone would see him the way he wanted to be perceived, but inside he was depressed, inside he hurt, inside he was alone. Inside his mask was a kid reaching out. I just sat in the bleachers of the gym crying. Tears ran down my face and they didn't stop. It had hit me too close to home.

Some of the students approached Jeremy when he was done and told him he should come and talk to me. Incredibly, he did just that. I didn't say a word to him, because I wasn't ready to talk. Everyone else, from the doctors to the physical therapists, who'd tried to make me whole again had failed. I looked at Jeremy Kingsley and saw just another person like them. Totally unfair, I know, but I'd lost faith in the ability of others to find the magic bullet I couldn't find.

But I hadn't lost faith in myself. Not at all; I just kept everything bottled up inside. When I wasn't racked by pain, I was thinking about it. During my sophomore year at Eastern High School, I finally opened up to a girl in my biology class, Rasha. She asked me why I was limping. I told her it was just swagger, but she kept pushing and pestering me about it, until about three months into the school year I finally told her everything. She thought I was crazy thinking I wasn't normal, and what was the big deal about being so good at sports anyway, she asked me. I didn't respond to her question but managed a smile to thank her for being candid without being condescending or cruel. Maybe this was that sign I was looking for, that things were about to turn the corner. Then, two weeks later, Rasha was stabbed to death by her father because she was pregnant.

I was at school and one of her friends who lived next to her told me the news, before we entered the biology classroom that day. I was confused and devastated at the same time. I didn't see that coming at all. She was so nice, so pleasant to me, like a sister almost. She was the first girl I had ever talked to outside of my own culture, and I was intrigued about where she came from and why she wore the clothes she did. She was also the first girl that I had talked to about my life and my struggle. She was beginning to understand me and who I was. I felt robbed in a way, I felt lost, and even more confused about what just happened. I couldn't believe something like that could happen to such an innocent girl, how crazy this world was.

What on earth was going on, I wondered? I was at a loss for thoughts, my mind almost went blank. Poor Rasha had a whole life to live, and had such a kind spirit about her. It just seemed so unfair and, coupled with my own experiences, plunged me back into the doldrums of living a life that was clearly unfair and nothing like what I always thought it would be like.

Later in the year I opened up to an Asian girl. She saw that I was talking to Rasha, and she saw how I reacted when I found out the news of her death. I was tired of putting walls up around me and saw this as another opportunity to make a friend I could open up to. All we did was talk, mostly about Rasha, since we were kindred spirits as far as her tragic passing went.

But I guess some people got the wrong impression about the nature of our relationship, because not long after we became friends, a gang of her brothers, cousins, and their friends jumped me in the hallway, wielding chains, bats, and even a butterfly knife. I was just minding my own business, heading to basketball practice. I'd opened up to that Asian girl about lots of things, but not about my martial arts training.

When they pounced on me, I sidestepped the knife, blocking the incoming thrust with an outward block. Then I took a small, powerful step forward and hit the knife-wielder smack dab in the face. The second guy swung the baseball bat he was holding in a long, looping motion. I ducked, and the bat hit the wall of the stairs. Then I clambered down the stairs, striking him with an elbow to the back of the head. There were still two more of the Asian kids waiting for me, coming up toward me One had a chain and the other was holding something I thought were nunchucks. Halfway down the next flight, I flung myself over the railing and landed directly behind them. There was another figure holding a bat standing by the door. He swung it at me. I ducked beneath the blow and used his own momentum to shoulder him out of my way, so I could make a beeline outside and lit out into a mad dash toward the gym 200 yards away, where basketball practice would soon start.

I thought I'd come out of the scuffle untouched, until I looked down and saw that the knife had slashed my forearm and I was bleeding. I looked at my other arm and saw it was scuffed up as well. I guess I didn't feel it when it happened—my adrenaline was still pumping, my endorphins were flowing. I was on the high, but the crash of reality was soon to hit, likely before I got to basketball practice. I never talked to that Asian girl again, but bad things continued to swirl around me.

Not long after my encounter with the Asian gang, a fellow basketball player named Letwan was stabbed to death on a train. It could've been random, or it could've been related to a different gang. Taken together, these two incidents kind of exemplified the fact that I'd lost my trust in people. Shedding the crutches hadn't shed the scars left by the way people had treated me for the all those months and years I had to crutch my way around, my "cripple" period. I was always watching my back, no idea what was lurking behind the next corner. After so often longing to be around people, now I found myself alienated and isolated.

That descending spiral my life was on took me away from God and I started to believe that I was destined to never be happy or whole. I started to think that He wasn't on my side; why else could He let bad things keep happening to me? I began to think I needed a fresh start. What would life be like among new people, who didn't know me as the kid with crutches who squeaked down the hall? What would life be like if I got to start over?

I was about to find out.

What You Can Learn from This...

1. Bullies are all over the place. We need to realize that they feel the same things we do as the target. They feel emptiness inside somewhere, and they are also suffering from something.

2. Sometimes a fresh start is something we need. Most times, leaving your past to make a future is worth the pain of leaving the familiar.

3. Holding on to pain can bring more problems; being open and feeling vulnerable can actually become your strength. You just have to weather the storm.

CHAPTER 5

A Fresh Start

Lansing, Michigan; 2000

The process started when I switched high schools, enrolling for my junior year in Lansing Christian School, values-based school that offered an entirely different environment, where I could be looked at as normal, like everybody else. Even though I'd shed the crutches and braces and was coming into my own as a basketball player, people at my old school still looked at me as if I was still wearing them. They'd branded and defined me in a way I couldn't shake off no matter how hard I tried. I needed to make the switch in order to be branded a whole different way, based on the person I was now, instead of the one I'd been. Day one of the rest of my life.

I needed to a school where I wasn't afraid that I'd be jumped or attacked. But the transition was difficult in other ways. I had left a Class A school with a thousand students per class for a school that averaged only around thirty-five. Imagine the contrast in trying out for the basketball team my junior year, competing against a few dozen prospective players, compared to closer to a hundred back at my old school. My new potential teammates knew who I was, that I came from a super big, and well-known, program. So reputation preceded me, as they say.

And that turned out to be not such a good thing.

"I don't want you on my team," Coach Keith Ingles told me. "I know where you came from and I don't want you bringing it in here."

He was talking about my reputation for being super flashy, favoring behind-the- back passes and getting the crowd pumped up. Coach Ingles was old school. The very first day I walked into my new school, he came up to me before I even tried out and read me the riot act. His team, his rules, and I had no choice but to go along. But I also knew I could help make this a better squad.

"Look, you need me on this team," I told him. "We both know that. And all I want to do is play basketball."

Coach Ingles mulled it over and gave me a chance. Grudgingly. True to my word, I ended up playing every single position on the court, from point guard to center. The only battle between us was over which brand of basketball I'd be playing: the flashiness bred of all those driveway hoop battles with my brother, or the more staid, controlled player that went diametrically against my nature. And it's hard to change your nature at seventeen and a junior in high school.

One game, I threw one of my patented behind-the-back passes that caught a teammate by surprise and hit him right in the face. Coach Ingles pulled me for the rest of the quarter. Whenever I did anything that was even remotely flashy, drawing oohs and ahs from the crowd, he'd take me out, even if I hadn't done anything wrong. It was hard to play within a system and be myself at the same time. It was my identity versus the team's identity in Coach Ingles' mind, but I honestly believed they could coexist, if he just gave me a chance.

Students at my new school had no idea what I'd been through, before I transferred. And in my second hour there I walked into a classroom and I had one of those moments that changes your life forever. It's funny because this was just a teacher's aide class taught by the choir teacher, whose name was Layton De Vries. He had these soft blue eyes and always seemed to be smiling. He wore thin glasses that made those blue eyes seem like they were twinkling. But he also had the look of an athlete, six feet tall with broad shoulders.

This guy was a special kind of man. He was the same age as my brother Cass, early twenties, and had just gotten married to a beautiful woman and landed a good job in his field of choice. He actually reminded me a little of Cass, and the closeness in our ages allowed me to relate really well to him. I found myself, almost immediately, able to talk to Layton about anything. His personality was genuine. He was the teacher that everyone wanted to talk to and the one that everyone would remember after they graduated. That one teacher who makes a special type of impact in your life.

Layton's devout faith was something that immediately impressed me. He loved God and felt he'd been saved by Jesus, a man whose faith was the cornerstone of his life. And when we talked, he seemed to honestly care about all I'd been through. We talked about everything, from my childhood growing up to why I transferred. Everything. We'd talk while I set up the chairs for his choir class. Since that took only five minutes, though, we had time left to really get to know each other, even adjourn to the gym to play some Horse. I saw in him not just an adult who believed in me, but also a role model. Someone I could emulate and who came to exemplify the fresh start I was after, even more so because his presence was what steered me toward God and my own faith.

A crucial demarcation point.

Layton was interested in what I had to say, what I was going through, and what my past had been like. He talked to me about how holding things in and bottling things up only make things worse, because they make you dislike yourself—the person you need to believe in the most. I'm not even sure I ever used the term self-esteem back then, but I was clearly suffering from a lack of it. My talks with Layton De Vries, along with the friendship we built, began to change that.

I told him about the physical pain I experienced every day. I told him about all the repressed anger I felt toward those who'd hurt me, how I was going to use that for motivation to prove all those haters wrong. I told him all about my hip problem and how that had kept me from having a normal childhood, and how I didn't feel normal, even now. I told him about my sleepless nights, about how the pain in my leg made it feel as if my bones were made of hot coals.

I'd finally found a mentor, a confidant. Layton was the assistant basketball coach under Keith Ingles as well, so I saw him for about five hours every school day. And the whole time he was helping me learn who the new me was, we weren't alone; God was always with us and I was developing a relationship with Him at the same time. I got Layton hooked on Sprite, my drink of choice. I bought him one every day, and we'd drink our matching cans while going over basketball plays and talking through the offensive and defensive sets. We'd argue about who was the greatest of all time and did plenty of trash talking and joke telling along the way.

During choir class, he was always encouraging and made me sing as low as possible since, he quipped, I had an awful voice! He was right, of course, as I'd later learn when I sang that duet with my brother.

"Patrick," he'd say, trying to be positive, "you're the only one who can hit that note. There's a reason for everything."

I even talked to Layton about girls—hey, I had to talk to somebody, right? And this was one subject I figured I'd spare my big brother. I asked Layton about the girl who I was trying to ask out at the time, and he would give me pointers on how to just be myself and how she probably wanted to see the softer side of me, wanted to know what I was feeling. He talked about how he'd met his wife at college and how their new marriage was going. I told him how the father of the girl I liked already hated me and how he'd made that known after one of our games. He knew the school I had come from and had already confronted me with the likes of, "I know the kind of kid you are and you aren't welcome around my daughter."

Kind of kid I was? Huh?

Layton and I had a talk about this and how to handle it. I didn't know what to do so I went to him. He said if I truly liked this girl, I should get to know her more and share my life with her, to express my feelings instead of holding them back. He'd talk about how God would be there with me, and how I only thought I'd been alone through all the bad times when, in fact, He'd been with me the whole time. I just didn't know it. But, thanks to Layton, I knew it now. After that, he asked me if he could sing me a song, of all things, that for something like this he could express his thoughts best via music.

"Sure," I said, even though I really wasn't, at least not until I heard the actual words, which went like this:

> *How long oh Lord will you forget me forever?*
> *How long oh Lord will you refuse to show your face?*
> *How long must I wrestle with my own thoughts?*
> *How long must my heart be an empty place?*
> *O Lord how long, how long, oh Lord how long?*
> *How long will you give my enemy triumph?*
> *Look down, oh Lord, give an answer to my call.*
> *Show me hope, or I will breathe my last breath.*
> *And my foes will come rejoicing when I fall.*
>
> *But I have trust in your unfailing love.*
> *I rejoice in your saving power.*
> *I will sing and dance and laugh forever.*
> *You are with me in my darkest hour.*
> *You are with me in my darkest hour.*

Words that were just what the doctor ordered figuratively, and what the real doctors hadn't been able to provide in the literal sense.

The best thing about Layton was that he made me feel normal. I felt confidant and I finally had someone to open up to about things I'd never really shared with anyone. It almost felt as if it wasn't just the muscles in my bad leg that had atrophied under that cast; my feelings and emotions had been stunted as well, their progression retarded to the point where, until my discussions with Layton, I hadn't really caught up. All those taunts I'd endured about being a cripple made it easy to miss the fact that my real problems cut deeper, to the core emotional level. Layton had finally peeled back the surface to expose that, and he was that guy we all need in our lives, the guy who makes you realize who you are and what you're capable of.

One morning, I walked into the choir room with two iced Sprites in my hand and the copies already done for Layton's lesson of the day. He wasn't there, and the door to his inner office was locked. He'd felt fine the day before, so I went into the administrative office, only to learn they didn't know where he was either. Just then, I mean as I was standing there, they got a telephone call saying that Layton had been in an accident and had been hospitalized. It was, by all accounts, very serious, even grave. Looking at the school secretary, as she listened to the report, was enough to tell me what I'd learn later for sure.

I knew he was gone, that I'd never see him again.

My heart dropped. I felt something like a weighted cloud pushing me down. Everything inside me was screaming. I was shaking and my body instantly turned hot and sweaty. I walked out of the office and turned to go into the basketball gym. Tears started rolling down my cheeks like little rivers dripping down off my chin. I went into the boy's locker room and started to punch the lockers with everything I had. My knuckles were bloody from the repeated blows. Every one of those lockers in the back corner of the locker room was dripping blood, bent in and dented all around, looking like someone had taken a baseball bat to them.

Releasing my anger on that metal hadn't made me feel any better, and after ten minutes I sat down in the shower room in a pool of my own blood. I thought about the young teacher who'd become my best friend, and I knew I was never going to be able to talk to him again. He had been taken from me, in the midst of his own new beginning as well, his whole life ahead of him with his wife, Heidi. He was gone, the only guy who knew all my secrets and accepted me for who I was.

That morning, December 8, Heidi had gotten a phone call from Layton. He had slid on a patch of ice on his way to work and was sitting in his car in a ditch waiting for the tow truck. He was telling her how worried he was that he'd be late for work. Suddenly, in the middle of the conversation, the cell phone service went out.

An hour later, Heidi finally called the police station to see if everything was all right. The police informed her that there had been a second accident. A pickup truck had hit the same patch of ice and the back of the truck had slammed into the driver's side of Layton's car.

He was transported to Spectrum Health in downtown Grand Rapids with injuries to his legs, aorta, spleen, and head. His wife and family reached the hospital as fast as they could. Though hope prevailed during Layton's first day in the hospital, it became clear that he wasn't going to recover from his critical injuries. The doctors explained that the injuries to the aorta and the brain were each life threatening on their own. Taken together, they left no possibility for recovery. His family spent four days at the hospital, hoping for a miracle, praying and remembering.

Then, at 11:59 on Monday night, Layton's brain waves ceased and, in the presence of his family, he was pronounced dead. The family members were happy that most of his body was able to help so many others who needed his vital organs. Layton's death gave life and hope to many others, and yet, it left a massive hole in my heart.

I was so mad, so angry, that no one could talk to me. This kind of pain was worse than any of the physical pain I'd experienced with my hip. I wouldn't, *couldn't*, talk to anyone. I had just been getting close to him, finally had an adult with whom I could share my innermost thoughts and feelings. But now I was right back where I started, still racked by physical pain but now feeling emotionally, as well as spiritually, drained and pissed off with the same God Layton had encouraged me to draw closer to.

Then a wave of tortuous guilt washed over me for thinking of my own grief ahead of Heidi's and the rest of Layton's family. How small I felt in that moment. I knew I needed to push forward, but every time I tried to let go and focus on the things Layton would've wanted me to focus on, I hit a brick wall. My struggles didn't seem to matter anymore, all the battles I'd been striving so hard to win with Layton's help and counsel rendered moot. I didn't even want to think about moving on and forward. Instead, I wallowed in grief, sadness, and anger with God.

"Hey," I said to Him, "you know I can do this, I can do this on my own. I don't need your help to have me do what I want to do to get through life. I know you're there and I believe you know what you're doing to me in my life. I've already been through enough—why do you have to give me one more thing that I have to deal with?"

My heart felt stone hard and I could never envision opening up to anyone again the way I had with Layton, not if it meant going through this again.

A week later our choir class sang at his funeral. It took every bit of willpower I had not to cry, because I was teetering on an emotional edge. I could have broken down at any minute and wept loud enough for everyone in the church to hear. So I bottled that sadness up, held onto it, and pushed it as far down as I could. Layton was gone, he wasn't coming back, and I didn't know how I could go on without him.

His obituary read:

LAYTON REID DE VRIES was born March 17, 1976, and he died December 11, 2000. He was a friend, brother, son, husband, child of God, and a great teacher to have.

During his funeral I couldn't bear to look up at anyone, so I walked over to his coffin and cried silently so that none of the other students would see me as the same weak and frail kid so well known at my old school. I watched and listened as Heidi sang a song, the same song Layton had sung to me about that darkest hour.

Indeed.

My grief gave way to an intense anger over never getting the chance to say good-bye. I didn't get to thank him for his friendship, or tell his wife about the surprise hot air balloon ride he was going to take her on, to let her know that his love for her gave him wings like an angel's, not realizing he was just months away from doing so all by himself. I never wanted anyone to get inside my mind or my heart again. No friend, no brother, no family member, no girls. *No one!* I built an even bigger wall before me, because it was easier to live behind it than make myself face the world.

I remember getting in a fight with a guy from Bellevue High. I hit him so hard, he landed facedown in the snow, and I just walked away. I thought he deserved it, because of his loud mouth and his trash talk about my school and the girls there, whom he called names I won't repeat here. So I felt justified in hitting him, and anything and everything else to vent my rage. Felt justified to scream, yell, cry— anything but cope. All that physical pain I'd endured over the years, and now it was emotional heartache that was destroying me.

Layton's death brought me to a dark, dark place where I didn't like anything anymore, nothing at all. Not people, not school, not sports—nothing. Maybe this was another test for me to prove myself. To show God I understood His plan by playing basketball in college, then in the pros, and maybe even become a gold medalist in the decathlon event for the United States of America at the Olympics. After all this, God must've had something much bigger in store for me, right? Why on earth else would my physical pain now be matched by a agonizing emotional angst that left me feeling empty inside?

Similarly, though, why on earth would I think that I knew what's better for me than God does? Maybe it was because I didn't have the kind of personal relationship with Him that Layton was urging me to build. I wasn't living for Him and for something bigger than myself. A terrible lesson to learn, rendered even more painful by the fact that Layton's death had proven me woefully behind in heeding the lessons he'd tried to teach me. And until I heeded those lessons, I'd never be healed in mind, body, or spirit.

From the wrenching pain that came to dominate my life in the wake of Layton's passing, that small tidbit of realization began to blossom. Ultimately, I would use my best friend's death as a motivator, as a stimulus to live my life in a way that lived up to his example.

Ultimately.

The short term was something else entirely. About six months after Layton's death, I was getting ready to start senior year in high school. And the rocky relationship that I had with Coach Ingles, previously tempered at least somewhat by Layton's patience and wisdom, began to deteriorate even further. Just a few years back, I would've given anything to be running and jumping, never mind trying to lead my high school team to a state championship. Now my perspective had grown stilted to the point where the remarkable recovery I'd managed physically was blunted by my own ego and selfishness.

Coach Ingles and I both knew we needed each other this upcoming season. It was his job to come up with the system and mine to make it work. He even made me captain, showing me more regard than I gave him.

The problem was I had to do everything his way and that infuriated me. Clearly, I hadn't learned the lessons of Layton's death yet and, just as clearly, doing so wasn't in the offing, as we drew closer to the season's start. My coach and I got into plenty of arguments after practice and after one game, late in the season, we had a total falling out. We started screaming at each other in the locker room. I was beyond furious over his sitting me out the entire first quarter and the third. How was I supposed to lead our team to the district title by playing only sixteen minutes in the game?

We lost by a few points to a team I knew we could have dominated, if the coach hadn't been out to get me since the day I got to that school. He told me it was to prove the point that I wasn't the answer, that he didn't need me in order to win, that I didn't belong on the team, and I didn't know how to be a teammate. I stormed out of the locker room that night like a hurricane.

Later that week I got a call from a rival coach. He told me that he'd nominated me for All-state, but that Coach Ingles said no, he wasn't going to support that effort and said he'd go as far as making sure I wasn't even considered. Soon after I learned about this, I got a moment after school to get him alone and let out all of the rage that was bottled up inside. All the other kids were gone, so it was just the two of us. And we were arguing so badly and yelling so loud, I'm sure anyone who may still have been around was left wondering what was going on.

I told him what I'd found out from that rival coach, and he didn't bother denying it. We got into a screaming match and it took all of my willpower not to physically unleash the rage that was clawing at me from the inside, trying to get out. Although I was able to hold it in, I couldn't hold my tongue.

"I wish you were dead!" I raged at him, years of frustration spilling out in a moment I regretted almost immediately.

I didn't even recognize myself anymore, could hardly picture saying something like that to a true enemy, much less an adult who enjoyed the very same goal I did. What would Layton have thought about that? It wouldn't have happened if he'd been there, I told myself, but he wasn't and the burden fell on me now to stop wallowing in self-pity and selfishness. I went back later to apologize, but Coach Ingles had already left, so I went back to see him first thing the next morning. Mend the fences. Make everything all right again and commit myself, as captain, to setting a much better example for my teammates.

He wasn't in his office down by the boy's locker room, so I headed up to the computer lab where he taught the typing and computer class for the high school. I opened up the set of doors, and that's when I saw him there with Ms. Iverson. He was lying on the floor. His lips were blue, his face ghastly pale, and Ms. Iverson was giving him mouth-to-mouth. I jumped in to help try and resuscitate him, but it was no use. Coach Ingles had suffered a heart attack that morning before school started, and would be dead before he reached the hospital.

I had gotten my wish. And it felt like I'd killed him myself.

What You Can Learn from This...

1. Your tongue can cut through people like knives. The words that you choose could haunt you forever, so be quick to listen, and slow to speak and slow to become angry.

2. We have all done wrong and have fallen short from the glory of God. He is always with us even in our darkest hour.

3. If you don't forgive yourself, or forgive others, then your heart will find its path to darkness, hardened and black.

CHAPTER 6

The Darkest Hour

Lansing, Michigan; 2002

"I wish you were dead."

Those words still haunt me to this day. Plenty had led up to that moment, all of it birthed in the inner turmoil wrought by my believing I'd been a victim too long, all I'd gone through leaving me feeling entitled and not always in command of my emotions. My coach and I had yelled at each other so loud before I'd wished him dead, I vividly recall both of us slinging spittle from our mouths. He was as stubborn and set in his ways as I was, neither of us giving an inch.

But what I wouldn't give to take back my final words to him. I wake up at night still, reliving that moment in a pool of my own sweat. I felt solely responsible for his death and for ruining his career and leaving his wife alone. I left his sons without a father and I left the school with another friend, teacher, and coach to replace. This was an unspeakable tragedy, and it was all my fault. Sure, my conscious mind told me that was ridiculous. Saying something, wishing something, doesn't mean it's going to happen; if it did, I would've been able to wish myself back to normal all those years I spent housebound. That, though, didn't at all lessen the pangs of guilt that plagued me.

This was someone, after all, whom I'd had a personal relationship with, someone I saw every day. Sure, we didn't see eye to eye; I had my way and he had his. I thought he was stuck in his ways, and he wouldn't budge, but I was the one who pushed it too far, I was the one who yelled first, I was the one who said those wretched words. And those words haunted me in ways I can't possibly describe. Feeling that bad, and that guilty, left me thinking about the physical pain I continued to experience, as if the emotional pain racking me wasn't bad enough.

During my senior year in high school, there were days where I hurt so much from running, exercising, or just moving around a lot that the next morning I'd have to call my mom to help me out of bed. It got so bad at times, all I could do was remain lying down and find the most comfortable position to put my leg in so that I wouldn't cry and scream in agony. There were days after basketball practice when I would talk to my head coach and tell him that I hurt so bad that I couldn't take the bus to the games. When my dad could make my games, I would lay down in the back of his van, so that I wouldn't have to deal with the pain stemming from sitting for an even brief period on those stiff, cramped seats.

But my desire to prove people wrong by showing I could be the best trumped all else, so much so that I was willing to sacrifice walking the day following a game. Succeeding and excelling against all odds became an obsession for me. If I made ten shots, I wasn't happy because I thought I should have made eleven.

I was sorry for a lot of things in the wake of Coach Ingles' death to fulfill my cursed wish, and I also thought I'd let God down. I'd come to accept that He had given me a disability so I'd have to learn how to endure the pain, to make determination my most important ally. At the same time, having to overcome a disability left me humbled in the face of the dedication it took to, not just be good enough, but the best. The surest recipe to avoid the kind of arrogance I displayed in front of my coach during our final, fateful meeting. Doctors had told me what I was achieving as a high school senior was impossible.

But the impossible is only that because it hasn't been done yet, just like sports records are meant to be broken.

You can do this, I'd tell myself.

Still, having two coaches, people you're close to, die in two years is tough for a kid, tough for anyone. Keith Ingles was a good guy and a good coach, a great husband and a father. We'd started to develop a relationship before that big argument and, in retrospect, I think he was hard on me because he wanted to make me better. Just like he had made me a captain my senior year and built an offense that left the primary scoring responsibilities with me. What else did I want; what else was I expecting?

This proved to be a real turning point in my life, because it made me question the kind of person I was. Good people didn't treat people the way I treated Coach Ingles. Good people didn't cause the deaths of people important to them or, at least, wish them dead. You're not going to see eye to eye with everyone about everything, and you can't go around wishing all the people you don't agree with dead. That's true about all aspects of life, including school and business. I started to realize all I'd been through as a kid had left a formidable chip on my shoulder that had only hardened by the time senior year rolled around.

I don't know, maybe I was just scared of what was to come and maybe I didn't want to confront the fact that I wasn't going to be good enough to play pro basketball, maybe not even good enough to play college ball for a decent program. And I think, in part anyway, I blamed Coach Ingles for holding me back, not giving me the freedom to excel when the truth was I'd hit a wall in my talent level because there was only so much I could do to overcome my average size and lingering physical challenges. My response to that was to lash out at the one person who was trying to help me find the door built into that wall.

As my senior year in high school wound down, that realization made me feel a lot of things, but mostly it made me want to be better, to find what I'd lost with the death of my coach and prove that I could be a better person. I graduated in the spring of 2002 in aimless fashion, though, rudderless as I looked toward my future. I got more than a few offers to play ball at Division I, D-II, and D-III schools. I visited a few colleges in my surrounding area, but I didn't want to go to college just to go, and I was talking with a few basketball coaches about playing ball at a smaller school to improve my value at a bigger one. But it was still a toss-up as to what I wanted to do, as well as what I should do. I had lost the passion to go for the dream that once had me shooting a thousand three-pointers a day.

Ultimately, I settled on a college but, even once the decision was made, it just felt wrong and I ultimately opted not to accept the spot they were holding. My father looked at where I was at in my life and sought to bring me into his network. He wanted me to follow in his footsteps to become an IBO (Independent Business Owner) with the Amway Corporation. So I went in and signed up. I learned about the business and met some great people, hardworking individuals who made a terrific team. Jim Guldberg was a great mentor to my father and to me, along with many others I crossed paths with. This was an amazing opportunity, and I saw how well the system worked, how American it was—free enterprise at its best, with the sky as the only limit to how much you could make or how far you could go.

I enjoyed my time with Amway and could see myself making a life and career out of it, just as my father had. But I kept hearing this voice in my head telling me to do the impossible. I needed to find a purpose, an anchor, something to ground me in a way where I could build the foundation to become the kind of man I knew I could be. So much of my life up until this point had been about overcoming, and I started to realize that had been the case for so long, it had come to define me. I suppose I could've been happy making a career out of Amway, except my unusual childhood had left me with a different definition of what happiness was, and I started to suspect that I wasn't going to find that with the company.

I needed to turn my attention to achieving, to thriving instead of merely coping. To getting ahead instead of staying even. And I knew that going into business with my father wasn't going to help me achieve that. Just more of the same: me allowed to continue being who I already was, the person who had wished a man to his death. But I didn't want to be that person; I wanted to be somebody better, somebody more, the best in my own eyes and everyone else's. I wanted to make a difference for people who couldn't defend themselves. My boyhood experiences, all that I'd had to overcome, left me with a keen appreciation of what it was like to feel helpless, to need to rely on others. My future needed to be based on never feeling helpless again.

I needed to be one of those "others." I didn't want to stand out. I didn't want to be a millionaire. I didn't want to have fame and fortune or wear the latest fashion. I wasn't motivated by money. Money may make the world go round, but my heart was set on something different, something impossible. I figured I owed God that much and asked for His guidance, His help. And not long after I was struck by a realization, a visceral sense of what I was meant to be and what God had been preparing me for all along:

I am a warrior. I need to serve.

I wanted to make a difference in the best way I knew of, and that would be by becoming a warrior defending this great nation and trying to follow the route that God had set in motion for me I was only just seeing. I read a letter that my dad had written to my uncle in a time of great emotional pain and suffering, and this helped me to understand what it was like to hope for the best, get the worst, and trust God through it all to keep going and never give up.

His hand is on the little fellow's shoulder as the two walk onto the dusty baseball diamond on this warm June morning in 1962. There are lots of others boys there with their dads and some are dressed much finer than others in uniforms that were either bought brand new or handed down by brothers. But the little 7 year old who walks onto the field now is dressed in pants way too big for him which his mom has sewn in obviously too many places. A shirt from who knows where, probably the Salvation Army, and an old worn-out cap that's red. His little shoes are torn at the edges and he's also small for his age. This smallishness is exaggerated too, by the big ball glove on his left hand, a hand-me-down or one he found in some obscure box or trunk in his upstairs room at home.

That's how my dad opened his letter to my uncle, reflecting on the death of my brother Cameron. But the little boy in the story was him, his own youth recalled in a time of unspeakable tragedy. The letter concludes like this:

On July 30 and 31 of 1981, Rod Bisher came close to giving up and quitting. But because faith in God has always been first and foremost since he became a Christian and because from 2,400 miles away another man who once threw footballs and baseballs to me to catch and to hit and to throw, and who had experienced death before his eyes in Vietnam, and in the loss of a wife, and has experienced hope and love in a wonderful son, an echo came from the recesses of my heart and mind that said, "Rod, don't ever give up and don't you ever quit. I did not quit. Cameron may have a chance. If not, God has him in His mighty hands. I'm praying for him." Thanks, Dan. Thanks for the hand on the shoulder.

The PS reads, "I hit two home runs last week."

Reading those words, expressing unconditional love and attachment, resonated with me in a way few things ever had, filling me with a sense of responsibility to be worthy of all my parents had done and sacrificed so I could be whole again. There's great dignity in pursuing a career in a business, but I had to believe that my finally shedding my crutches and leg braces was toward a greater and more selfless purpose. I felt more obligated to do what I could, to not give up, and to make my mother and father proud. I didn't want them to feel guilty about having to support another child who just brought them more pain and harder life circumstances. I wanted to be great in their eyes. To give them something that would make them proud of their youngest son, something that would make up for all the years they'd played nursemaid for me and later endured the snide remarks and glares that had hurt them even more than they hurt me. All that had been out of my control, but now *I* was in control.

And yet this period was a real struggle for me. I didn't end up going to college. I backed out and decided not to accept offers from several schools that wanted me to play basketball for them. The deaths of Layton De Vries and Keith Ingles had stolen the love of the game from me. By the end of my senior year, after I'd wished Coach Ingles dead, I was just going through the motions on the court. Sure, I love competition and I love beating people—winning. Basketball was my first love, but not my true passion. Finding myself meant pursuing more than that. I felt compelled and called to do something more, to serve. To keep pushing, to keep trying to find myself.

I didn't know what I wanted but I knew there was something more out there for me. Basketball was a means to go to college, but I wasn't going to college. And staying in business with my dad wasn't the answer either. One night, I was on the roof of the house I'd grown up in, looking at the stars, when I heard a voice, barely audible in little more than a whisper.

"You are a warrior. You need to serve."

I felt in that moment that virtually everything I'd been through, had been preparing for that moment. Whether it was really God's voice or not, I was going to become a warrior for God, fighting a whole different kind of battle.

I ended up at a Naval recruiting station and made my decision then and there. I was going to enlist and become a Navy SEAL, my future as clear to me as what lay directly across the street.

Wait a minute, not so fast. My friends were skeptical, to say the least.

"Navy SEAL? Don't even try it, man!"

"Really think you're cut out to be the best of the best?"

"I don't know, man; I think you might be dreaming a little too big, even for you."

My dad didn't exactly jump on the bandwagon either.

"Are you sure?" he asked me. "I don't question your desire, but what about your hip?"

The thing about my dad was that when I'd try to do something new or even the least bit risky, I could see the fear in his eyes of what might happen. He didn't want to see me back on the couch again, didn't want me to risk suffering the kind of repeat injury I might not be able to recover from. I thought I could see the loss of Cameron lingering, plaguing him. I'd always been able to notice the moments that slipped by both of my parents when they would slide out of reality and think about my late brother. As if they were in a dream and could see his face right in front of them. Where he was still alive and we were a complete family. I'd watch them stunned by the picture of him hanging on the wall in our living room, eyeing it with a dreamy but sad expression that asked, "What if?" The moments when they would lose it and cry after seeing his face captured in a frame. My mother couldn't get through cleaning the room after dusting off his photo, so she would cry while gazing at his picture.

I'd watch from the corner of the room that led to the dining room, wondering what I could do to help our family that was suffering and mourning a son who was taken too soon. I was helpless to give them what they needed. How can you fill a hole in the heart? You can't, it's there forever. Every time I winced in pain, I saw in my father's eyes that he was feeling the same pain I was, and the last thing he wanted was for me to subject myself to a situation fraught with the kind of risk I might not be able to walk away from. But I owed this to my parents, I owed it to myself to try. To make them feel as much pride for me, as the sadness they felt over the loss of Cameron.

My uncle, a Marine, said to me "Now, Pat, becoming a SEAL is almost impossible. The number of guys who don't make it through that program is staggering. I think you should listen to your father."

Of course my uncle Dan would say that; he wanted me to be a Devil Dog, a mean-mugging, muscle-bound, hard-hitting, lead-slinging Marine. Semper Fi, do or die! *Oorahh!* But I needed to chart my own path. I would become a Navy SEAL, because that was the best, the pinnacle, the tree I could no longer reach the top of after my hip finally betrayed me.

My grandfather agreed.

"Pitter Patter," he said, using the name he'd always called me, "I know you can do this. I've seen you do the impossible already, and if I'm not around when you make it through, I'm already so proud of you, so proud of what you've decided to do for this great country."

My grandfather was a great man. He fought against age and disease for as long as he could, and was indeed around when I became a SEAL. He passed away a few weeks later, but I know he's been with me since then and always will.

What I didn't know at the time, after I officially signed up, were that more setbacks awaited me along the road to becoming the man I always knew I could be.

What You Can Learn from This...

1. Saying things in the heat of the moment could ruin something that could be great. If I could have taken a step outside of myself and focused, breathed, and relaxed, things could have been different.

2. The choices you make in the most difficult times can make a better future for you, or keep you on the same path. Are you willing to make a path where you want to go, or continue the life paved by others?

3. Lessons can be learned by hard times, or they can be your excuses. Don't despise God's discipline and don't resent His reprimand, because He disciplines those He loves, as a Father He delights in His son and what he can become.

THE MAN

CHAPTER 7

BUD/S

There will be an exceptional few with burning desire who persevere when their bodies are screaming to quit, yet continue on. These men experience a tremendous sense of pride, achievement, brotherhood and a new self-awareness that, "I can do anything!!" The most outstanding among them—that man whose sheer force of example inspires his classmates to keep going when they're ready to quit—is the "Honor Man" of the Class.

–From NAVYSEALS.com

San Diego; Spring, 2006

I think experience, that entire ordeal as a young boy, prepared me for BUD/S (Basic Underwater Demolition/SEAL) training and the basic conditioning, boot camp experience that preceded it by a few months, starting in February of 2006. I enlisted in the Navy as a BUD/S candidate with a chip on my shoulder from the crutches and leg braces I'd shed once and for all to reclaim my life, though not my childhood. I had the sense that with all I'd been through, all the adversity I'd overcome, I could accomplish anything now.

Not always a good thing, since during boot camp it left me with a sense of defiance that led to my intentionally leaving my shirt untucked and my dog tags hanging out, so that I'd be forced to work out more. That passed for a punishment in the eyes of my instructors, but not in mine. I remember laughing out loud during the basic conditioning portion of boot camp when we were getting "beat" by doing flutter kicks, and someone said they needed to call an ambulance because he couldn't take the torture of the workout. We'd only been at it for ten minutes.

My fellow recruits called me "Preacher SEAL," because they knew I was a BUD/S candidate, and I'd pray for the group every night. It got to be quite the thing, a regular ritual. I still had a kind of love/hate relationship with God; hate because of what He'd put me through and love because of how He'd helped me overcome it. I'd become obsessed with doing everything on my own, gleaning from my childhood ordeal the lesson not to expect anyone to help you if you can't help yourself. But I'd also come to grips with the fact that no one achieves anything alone. I came to the realization that God had always been in my corner; He just wanted me to go the full twelve rounds and suffer a whole bunch of knockdowns, only to still be standing (literally) when the final bell rang. Becoming Preacher SEAL was my way of thanking Him, I guess. Spreading His word without then realizing how much I'd be turning to Him later on.

My RDC (Recruit Division Commander), Petty Officer Billingslee, yelled at me for running in the "Ship." That's the room you have to stay in with your fellow recruits, a big huge open bay area with a ton of bunk beds where you spend lots of your time in boot camp. It also contains a lot of other rooms, almost the same way a ship does. Hence, the name. I ran at night because I wanted to stay in shape for the BUD/S training. I passed every test, surprising everyone who'd gotten even a glimpse of my medical file when the call came from SR Chief (SEAL) Rhoads at the base that I'd reached the final stage of admission to BUD/S.

Given the physical issues with my leg that continued to linger, I couldn't afford even the slightest setback, if I was to fulfill my dream of becoming a SEAL, the best of the best. It all went back to that day I'd caught a glimpse of myself standing straight and strong while staring in the mirror. At that point of my life, I defined myself by all the things I couldn't do. Once I got better, I turned toward not just any goal, but a kind of ultimate goal. Becoming a Navy SEAL, even just trying to become one, meant I would be able to physically do *anything*, as opposed to virtually nothing. A whole new way of defining myself.

The most nerve-racking time came when I was called in for a prescreening during a naval doctor's visit to make sure I was fit for full duty to attend BUD/S. I remember praying to God and asking Him to help me out with my loftiest of goals, asked Him for a kind of payback.

Getting into the Navy was one thing, but being accepted into BUD/S was a whole other thing, and I was worried about the visit because this doctor, like several before him, held my future in his hands. It was either SEAL training or getting stuck with the likes of that guy who asked for an ambulance. I was after the chance of a lifetime, to test my physicality to the absolute limits to see if I had what it takes to be part of the greatest, baddest, hardest warriors anywhere.

I went into his office, my palms sweaty and almost trembling in anticipation. This guy sat in front of people all day in a position to determine the rest of their careers, their very fates. He knew me only as the name in the file before him, his eyes and mannerisms so robotic I half expected him to pause to change out his batteries. He looked over my file and nodded, his expression loosening and seeming to peer at me in a different way.

"Interesting," he said. "That's a very rare disease. I've heard of it, but you're the first person I've ever met who actually suffered from it. Who performed your surgery?"

I cleared my throat. "Doctor Robert Hensinger."

He jumped out of his chair, utterly flabbergasted. "I was his understudy for years!"

"He's a great guy," I said, excited myself now. "I'm only here because of him. He helped me get through this horrible disease with little to no issues. I feel no pain and I run five miles a day. I work out all the time and feel great."

Without posing a single other question, he approved my paperwork and continued to talk about his experiences working with the great Doctor Hensinger. First, Hensinger had given me a future. Now his mere name had secured it. Call that a coincidence if you want, but I'll never forget something I read in a book once:

Coincidence is another word for God.

The first day arriving at BUD/S, I walked into the room that I'd be sharing with two other candidates. The purpose of those few months of boot camp and basic conditioning was to militarize you as a person and take you out of the civilian mindset. But only a very small percentage transition into BUD/S, and I was lucky enough to be one of them.

While I unpacked that first day in May of 2006, out from the bathroom came Hood, wielding this huge SRK knife.

He looked at me with this really intense gleam and said, "They gave us knives!"

I thought this guy was crazy, that he might use the knife on me in my sleep to see how sharp it was. What had I gotten myself into? I figured I'd better get an answer to that question, at least as far as Hood was concerned.

"Okay, it's a knife. What's the big deal?"

"My last deployment," he explained, "my ship was on lockdown the whole time. They wouldn't let us have anything or go anywhere."

"Well," I picked up, "you were on a boat in the middle of the ocean in a combat zone. What did you expect?"

"I was hoping to end up here."

Hood, like most of the others in my class, was just trying to see if he had what it takes to meet the physical standards of BUD/S, test himself after being at sea for an extended period. I don't think he really expected to make it and he ended up quitting during the first phase and went to college instead. That was the thing about BUD/S, or any endeavor even remotely similar to which you commit yourself. You can only get out what you put in. If you don't think you can make it, you won't. I'd already learned that going in, the hard way. In that moment, all I could figure was that my childhood ordeal had prepared me for this moment. BUD/S wasn't about testing my mettle; BUD/S was about becoming a Navy SEAL.

Hood was like most of those who quit: a great guy with a great attitude, but it just wasn't meant for him. That's not a knock on him or his character; it's just a fact of a brutal training program in which only a few make it past the first phase before Hell Week even begins. My advantage was that I already knew hell.

There are snippets of BUD/S training on YouTube now, there are tons of books out there that describe it, and I think the Discovery Channel ran a reality show about it not too far back. But none of those capture the rigors of actually going through it on a day-to-day basis. Watch those shows and snippets, and you get the impression you only have to hold out and endure for one hour minus commercials. Those one-hour episodes only hint at the brotherhood of guys that you spend every hour of the day with through months of pain and torture.

I'm not going to give you a tell-all story about BUD/S, detail all of my experiences in it, or give you the code to crack BUD/S and become a Navy SEAL. But I do want to highlight my experiences as they pertain to never surrendering your goals or giving up on yourself or your dreams.

Everyone was on edge the first morning and no one knew what to expect about what was going to happen that day, no matter how much we had heard. At 4:30 in the morning on the first day of our BUD/S training, we all lined up into our assigned boat crews of six men each. The highest-ranking guy was designated leader, in keeping with the military's hierarchal chain of command. We lined up next to another boat crew with another on our other side, and so on. Then our leading petty officer told us that we weren't moving fast enough, and if we wanted to make it in this training, we'd have to be faster. Keep in mind this wasn't an actual BUD/S instructor, just our own group leader doing his job.

I was thinking, *Man, this guy is serious*, and I was glad to have him as our leader. Not so the guy next to me who clearly resented being ordered about by someone he perceived to be an equal or lesser. Alpha male–hood at its best.

"Screw this guy," he said, or something to that effect. "I'm not paying attention to this a-hole"

I swung toward him. "Dude, what's your problem, bro?"

I would've punched this guy in the face if he didn't stop mouthing off and being a dick to this leader of ours. I had an immediate distaste for him and then he got up in my face with these enraged eyes, ready to take his aggressions out on me now. Fine. I was ready to give it to this d-bag, even though he had to get up on his toes to even come close to looking me in the eye. Guy looked like a hobbit from the *Lord of the Rings* movies to the point where I wondered if he had those weird oversized feet squeezed inside his boots.

"You want to listen to this asshole, be my guest," he snarled. "He don't know shit. He's just old Navy, a goddamn petty officer who's probably washed out of this a half dozen times. That don't make him a leader."

I backed off and remembered why I was there, why I had joined, and what I was supposed to do.

"Whatever, dude," I said to him. "Maybe you're right, but I hope you're wrong. It can't be good for us if you're right."

I nicknamed the guy "Gotez." He explained that he knew what he was talking about because he'd been here before. He said that guys who boss others around disrespectfully and don't know how to deal with their teammates don't last more than a few weeks. He told me that in his former BUD/S class people like this tended to alienate everyone around them. They end up either dropping out themselves by ringing the infamous bell at any point of BUD/S training, or getting summarily dropped from training for being a turd.

For me, that bell was a symbol of everything I'd overcome to get to this point. It reminded me of the bell I'd ring to get my parents' attention when I was laid up on the hospital bed my parents had moved into the living room when I was recuperating from my first hip surgery. I had rung that bell a lot. But this one represented something else entirely, a submission to the kind of limitations I had steadfastly refused to concede to as a boy. As a man now, I had no intention of conceding, no matter what BUD/S threw at me. It was just too personal for me.

Sure enough, true to Gotez's word, our leader the petty officer quit two weeks later. He was typical of ninety-five percent of everyone else out there in society. He would've made a decent boss in business, making a solid living and raising a good family. He may have even been a great Leading Petty Officer (LPO) within the regular Navy. But the regular Navy, and the regular world, wasn't BUD/S and it wasn't the SEALs. That kind of mindset just doesn't work in this environment. You need to know how to deal effectively with people and with yourself. What to say, when and how to say it. How to pace yourself in any and all things. It all comes down to discipline. And for those who complain about the torture of being pushed to their limits for twenty or more hours a day, try spending a year of your life trading places between your bed and the couch. I would've given anything for this then and I'd still do anything for it now.

Gotez and I, interestingly enough, became the best of friends. We would joke around and tell funny stories to pass the time, and talk about our past and what it took to get to where we were now. We began a long-lasting relationship that is crazier than I can believe. Late nights at In-N-Out Burger were some of the best times I can recall on those rare occasions we broke from training. Up late cleaning our gear; talks about past fights; losses of loved ones and understanding pain from within. He lent me his car while he was at the island, a retreat in the Pacific where the third phase of BUD/S training took place. I stayed at his place all the time. Just a true brother in the whole sense. The dude would do anything for you and worked harder than anyone I have ever met. He pushed me to be the best I could be, and I pushed him right back. That's what the process was all about.

We were so cold one day when there was no sun, and it was so foggy you couldn't see across the street. We were on the pool deck, shivering and wet from the DECON shower that you have to walk through in order to enter the pool. Waiting for the instructors to come and destroy our BUD/S class for whatever we'd failed to do the previous day.

I was huddled up so close to Gotez that I could hear his heartbeat from his back. My ears and face were glued to his back, and my arms were wrapped around him. There was another guy behind me as well doing the same thing, and so on. We called that Nut-to-Butt, and I couldn't stop fidgeting, my thighs squeezed together.

"Do you have to pee?" Gotez asked me.

"Kind of."

"Just let it go, man. Like in that movie, *Dumb and Dumber*."

So I did. That's the cold, hard fact of BUD/S. If you are man enough to get peed on by another man, then you might be strong enough to make it through just the first phase of training.

First Phase is the toughest. It consists of 8 weeks of Basic Conditioning that peaks with a grueling segment called "Hell Week" at the midway point, where you'll be tested to your limits.

–From NAVYSEALS.com

That first phase was crazy on the hip, but everything else hurt too, like I was doing basketball two-a-days in high school again to prepare for the upcoming season. If you've ever been so sore that you can't stand up and everything locks up so tight you can't even move, you've got an idea of what I'm talking about. All you can do is sit there breathing and that's about it. Your abs are screaming at you, your arms and legs feel like Jell-O. Well, combine all of those at the same time and that's how I felt all day long, while being so cold I couldn't stop shivering on top of everything else.

I was on a two-nautical-mile ocean swim with some guy one day. I can't remember his name but I remember his face. The water was fifty-two degrees that day, and he was my swim buddy. That day we were going at a slow pace, slower than I wanted to but I needed to stay with him.

"Hey, hey, dude, I can't go anymore," he said out of nowhere, and popped his red flare and quit right in the middle of the swim.

A blessing in disguise for me, since anyone who'd quit in the middle of a swim was sure to quit on you when it really got rough. That's what you learn from the start in BUD/S: nobody makes it on his own, but everyone has to make it on *their* own. A crucial distinction.

After the first few weeks, people were dropping out like flies; just like the guy whose name I can't remember. I had no intention of dropping out at all. I wanted to get better in the water. I wanted to prove to the other guys who were ahead of me in the water or pool activities that I could pull my weight and then some. I found out you could get extra time on the weekend to get your skills up, so I did.

Like drown proofing, a vital drill where you have to perform various challenges with your feet bound and hands tied behind your back, including swim, stay afloat, and do various maneuvers. As a result, this part of the training regimen had proven to be the Waterloo for plenty over the years, and I was determined not to follow them. But me, Gotez, and another bud named Rob had a very hard time staying afloat with our hands and feet bound. We all had to work very hard just to keep our heads over the surface in order to breathe.

The more time I spent with these guys the more I admired them. I was amazed at their work ethic and astonished at how hard they were willing to push themselves to accomplish what seemed at the time an impossible task. Seeing Gotez fight for his own life in the water gave me the ability to try just as hard as he did. If he was capable of getting it done with his little hobbit body, then I sure wasn't going to let him show me up. I still had a huge chip on my shoulder that required me to prove I could do anything I set my mind to after years of not being able to do anything at all.

As time passed and things got really hard, BUD/S actually became more fun and rewarding. There were fewer of us now and that tightened the bond between us "survivors" even more. The harder we got pushed, and the more things sucked, the closer that bond became, to the point where none of us could imagine any of our number washing out and ringing the bell. You look at each and every one of these guys, my BUD/S brothers, as someone you can count on in the hardest times, and you want them to see you the same way. At the same time, you want the laggards to quit, so you don't have to carry their dead weight.

We were doing the Otter Run, named after one of our instructors and also known as the Seven Layers of Hell, in which Gotez again proved he was all heart. Step for step in what could best be described as full beast mode, he was one of the few of us who kept up with the lead instructor on the fastest run of first phase. During that run, Gotez told me to keep up no matter what, to be ready for anything without elaborating further.

So the first day, a Monday, we ran with instructor Otter and I was like, *That run wasn't that bad!* Gotez warned me to "just wait"—his words. Tuesday nothing and then Wednesday, it happened. In a blur like the Flash, Otter ran one direction up and down the giant sand berms, and then he suddenly made a turn in the opposite direction. I glimpsed Gotez through the other bodies running in four lines. He was on one side, and I was in the middle. He turned around, his head snapped, and he made eye contact with me and said just loud enough for me to hear, "This is it! Stay up front. Just get to the front." And he sprinted to the front of the pack.

I heeded his advice and followed, right behind Gotez, and it seemed like an impossible pace to keep up in the soft sand of Southern California berm hills. He looked back again to see my smiling face, as glad to see me as I was to be there. As we ran, I looked behind me to see the rest of the remaining BUD/S class scattered between fifty and two hundred yards back. Like me, they were heaving for breath, their legs burning and their chests feeling as if they were on fire.

Just as I was feeling like I should let up, I saw a picture in my mind of myself in leg braces and a body cast, crutches and physical therapy, tears, pain, struggle. Visions of my past gave me the boost I needed, enough to actually surge past Gotez. He looked me in the eye with the rage of a true warrior and let out a war cry, as if to say "Good job, brother!" Because that's what we were: brothers, soon to be laying down our lives for each other. Then he and I picked up the pace to chase down the next guy in front of us.

After about five miles, the instructor took off on us again, pulling well away from me, but not Gotez, who was clinging to his footsteps. I resolved to do the same and sure enough I closed the gap. The three of us were in a dead sprint for around three hundred yards or so, never letting up no matter how labored my breathing became and heavy my chest felt.

My legs were jelly and my lungs were burning hot coals. I was wheezing more than breathing, sounding like a panting dog. Things were getting hazy and I started focusing on each next step and no more. My goal was to stay up with Gotez, not to let him pull away. Then I heard screaming in the distance from behind us. I heard the staff yelling at the students, but I couldn't look back. Nothing mattered except what was ahead of me.

Finally I heard "Circle up!" and there were just five of us in the front of the pack with nearly a hundred and fifty behind us.

Gotez flashed me a smile, and it felt great to be there with the top performers, with the best, the mere opportunity for which had eluded me for so much of my childhood. Everyone else now had to earn the right to join us. Everyone else had to endure those Seven Layers of Hell, the series of events required to join us at the front of the pack, while we jogged casually in a small circle.

The first phase was wrapping up and we were inching closer to the feared and infamous "Hell Week." I was clueless on that subject, having come into BUD/S knowing very little about what awaited me in the hardest training known to man. Others, though, had talked to at least one current SEAL who'd gotten through it, and each of their Hell Week stories was more horrible than the next. Of course, the ones we didn't hear from were the ones who'd rung the infamous bell.

The bell meant nothing to me because I wasn't going to ring it. I could have rung the metaphorical bell so many times when doctors told me I wasn't going to walk, run, play sports again. The more people told me all the things I couldn't do, the more I wanted to push myself all the harder to prove them wrong. You don't know it's impossible if someone doesn't tell you. And it's been done before. Thousands of people have made it through BUD/S training. I just wanted to be a part of something greater than myself, prove that I could hang with others, find enough grit inside myself to never ring that bell the way I'd needed to ring an altogether different one back when I was a boy.

Most of the class had a sense of deep foreboding, if not outright fear, about what was to come, and those were the ones who all rang the bell at some point in the next week. Almost like they'd scared themselves out of succeeding. They'd lost before they even started.

But I'd already been through hell. They'd told me I'd never walk again, never mind swim. Never mind take part in BUD/S training, on the verge now of becoming a Navy SEAL I could taste it.

How bad could Hell Week be?

Bad enough to almost make me wish I was back on my living room couch.

Almost.

What You Can Learn from This...

1. When times get tough, only a few people in your life are there to stand by your side. Those are the people who really matter. Those are the only ones you can trust when the going gets tough.

2. The pain of quitting would have been worse than anything else, because all of my work would have been for nothing at all. There are always quitters in our lives, so do not be discouraged by what others feel they cannot do. It takes discipline, time, and harder work than any other person to reach your goals or dreams.

3. The fear of the unknown often causes people to fail before they even try.

CHAPTER 8

Setback

San Diego, California; 2006

"Boats on Heads" separates the men from the warriors, likely the most difficult training in all of BUD/S and a centerpiece of Hell Week. The weak get washed to shore and ring out.

During the week we had regular long, grueling night runs, and boat races with the boats either on our heads or with us paddling through the vicious surf. For me, everything was going along just fine.

Until it wasn't.

My boat crew and I were running on the sand with the boat bouncing on our heads when, all of the sudden, the boat began to sway back and forth. I was positioned in the two spot of the boat on the left side. There are six positions—one in the front, middle, and back—on two sides of the boat. The officer is usually in the middle in between everyone giving orders and steering the boat. He needs to be there to serve as the rudder, as six or seven guys running under a boat can be dangerous. Mr. Ball was that officer for us and he was not as outspoken as he should have been. His orders were fading in and out, and he was struggling to keep up with all of the sled dogs around him.

The fact that we were running for a mile with a boat on our heads, grinding away at the tops of our skulls like a meat tenderizer every time we took a step, was getting to him. I remember his body swaying back and forth. His feet were all over the place and his legs looked like Gumby trying to run. His arms dropped from the boat, and he was staggering lethargically about. He bumped into a guy on the right, and then came back over to our side. The man behind me pushed him back to center, but it was no use. He grabbed the edge of the right side of the boat and leaned to his left to try and stay up, but he lost control and couldn't stand to sprint in the soft sand any longer. When he lost control, I felt the boat come crashing down on my shoulder. I felt it rip out of its socket as the boat fell on me, with my arm left dangling and useless. I was twisted up and recall Senior Chief "Tush" grabbing my arm to check it out.

"Uh-oh," he said, to paraphrase the considerably more colorful language he used.

It was about the worst pain I've ever felt, and my thumb was literally facing the wrong direction. The arm was at a dead hang and it was out of the socket. I could feel the ligaments being pulled and ripped through the bone. I turned, rolled the shoulder, and then slid it back into the socket as best as I could.

The Senior Chief shined his flashlight into my eyes.

"Are you okay, bro?" he asked, the wariness evident in his voice. The fact that he went out of character to talk to me man to man, not student to instructor, felt surreal at that time.

"Hoo-yah, Senior Chief!" I responded, not about to risk saying anything that would set me back.

I tucked my arm into my life jacket and switched positions to the other side of the boat, so that I could use the other arm to continue helping my teammates. I could feel the tendons in my shoulder stretched into spaghetti-like strands, the tissue in my socket shredded. All I could think was that it hurt even more than the hip that had plagued my youth ever had. A group of instructors huddled up, got us to our positions, and named a new junior officer. The one who'd lost his balance quit shortly after that had happened.

But the damage had already been done.

Later that night I told Gotez how much pain I was really in, and he said to just suck it up until after Hell Week, and get it checked out then. He didn't want to see me get dropped for medical reasons, when I was this close to making it through. He always looked out for me and told me how it really was, and what I should do to be a better teammate. I learned that even if all odds are against you and nothing is going your way, all you have to do is keep going and never quit. Don't say "I can't" and don't dwell on the negative. Always look for the good and always find a way to turn something negative into a way to improve or adapt, so in time it will become a positive.

Easier said than done, in this case.

Hell Week, the culmination of the first phase of BUD/S training, consists of six days of nonstop training evolutions. It starts on Sunday. You only get two naps that are two hours apiece on Wednesday and Thursday, and you are done on Friday. Six days that feel like sixty, maybe even six hundred. That's why so few make it through. But I was determined not to be one of those, not to quit because of my bum shoulder. All the days and nights blended together. The chafing between my legs looked like uncooked meatloaf. My underarms hardly had any skin left. Whenver we entered the water, the burning of the salt would hit any part of the body that was unprotected due to lack of skin, growing us into warriors. Also each time, though, more of us would leave the water broken, the process eliminating the weaker-minded men around us, more and more of the original 214 that had started BUD/S training together dropping off.

Each minute felt like an hour and each hour a day. Boats on our heads and logs in our hands. Running over 110 miles in six days, wet and sandy. Being cold, wet, and miserable—it was all worth it when Friday's sunlight broke. Only a few more hours until we were going to be secured, and by midday Hell Week was over. Every guy who was still standing had earned their way one big step closer to becoming a warrior, even as phases two and three of the training process awaited us.

I felt like I had taken a big step, finally proven that I was tough enough to do it, just as tough as everyone else. That chip on my shoulder firmly in place, I was able to stand on my own two feet and show all the people who made fun of me, called me names like "Squeaky,' or baited me with taunts on the order of, "Run Forrest, run!" how wrong they were. Nothing motivated me more to become a SEAL than that.

I thought I was on my way and that I could even handle my shoulder issue, just as I had my hip. But then the lifesaving portion of training got me. My worst nightmare came true, because I had to rely on both my shoulders to swim out and then hold firmly onto the person I was trying to swim in to the side of the pool to simulate a surface sea rescue. Every time I'd pull an instructor to the edge of the pool and he tried to simulate a struggle and roll away from me, my left arm would actually pop out of its socket anew and I'd stop short of lifting him out. My lead instructor at the time gave me one last chance to pass with him, no more willing to see me fail than I was myself at this point.

"Show me you can do it!" he barked. "Show me you've got it in you!"

"Hoo-yah!" I coughed back at him in raspy fashion.

He wanted to see my all. He wanted to see what type of man I was, if I was comfortable in the water when things didn't go my way. He wanted to see if I had a warrior inside me. With water splashing about from his pretend struggles, I went in for the tackle. I got hold of him and started to pull him in. We wrestled, but I continued tugging him along. The two of us were literally strung together, when he barrel-rolled us. I tried to hang on, but my left shoulder ripped out of its socket yet again.

Damn!

I grabbed him with my right arm to hang on. We were at the bottom of the pool, separated by about six feet. That gave me the time I needed to put my arm back into its socket, grabbing and twisting it into position until I felt it click. The instructor tilted his head at me while we were both floating at the bottom of the pool, holding our breath, and pointed for me to rise.

"What was that?" he asked once we'd broken the surface of the pool, huffing for breath just like I was.

"My shoulder," I said, and told him what had happened during the Boats on Heads drill.

"Bisher, you stupid idiot!" he snapped as we climbed from the pool. "Get your butt to medical now!"

"I can do this!" I insisted. "I can tough it out and make it through."

"I know you're tough and I know you can make it through. But that," he added, pointing to my shoulder, "that needs to be fixed. Good thing, since I thought maybe you didn't have it in you to handle this lifesaving thing. Turns out you may be tough as shit, but you're also dumb as shit." He was grinning now. "Go to medical, then come back and tell me what they say there."

Turned out that the injury was much worse than I'd expected, and I was going to need surgery. Six anchors were attached to my tendons and muscle tissue, and a lift was put into my socket. Additionally, the doctor explained the bone had chipped off because of repeated trauma and dislocations; I'd suffered fifteen of them since the Boats on Heads mishap, culminating in the lifesaving drill in which I couldn't lift my instructor out of the pool.

I couldn't believe it. Another setback, my body betraying me yet again, the victim this time of pure bad luck that threatened to keep me from reaching my goals and prove everyone wrong yet again. I was used to people giving up on me, believing I had no chance. But I never gave up on myself and never considered failure an option.

Just like I knew I'd get rid of the crutches and leg braces, and not just walk, but also run again, so I was certain I'd triumph here.

I had to leave the class that I started with and wait until I healed up. Man, that hurt, a pain deep in my gut almost as bad as the one that flared constantly in my shoulder. I left all the guys I'd developed an incredible bond with and joined the ranks instead of others who were healing up. I thought I was going to feel like the little boy I'd once been, confined to his room or the couch downstairs. But that experience had taught me patience and persistence would win out. As long as I didn't quit on myself, I had the opportunity to recover and get back to full strength. I had willed myself back to health then, just as I would now and, again, would emerge stronger as a result. Sure, I'd watched others dropped from the program for issues far less serious than what I had, but they didn't share my past experiences.

And in that respect I discovered a new camaraderie with my fellow wounded candidates. I looked around and saw all the guys who were healing up, some I already knew and others I was about to. I was the new guy on the block, my rehab just beginning while theirs was more advanced. And they pushed me to my limits every day to be a better warrior. This group of misfits and broken dudes was labeled the "Rollbacks," composed of any SEAL candidate hurt during any of the three phases of BUD/S training. They, or "we" now, were held back and then "rolled" in when the next class reached the phase where we left off, once deemed physically able to do so.

In Rollback land, I prepared for surgery and prepped to stay strong. Shoulder surgery went as planned, and I was confident that I was going to bounce back. After all I'd endured, I viewed this as just another setback on a long road of them. Nothing was going to stop me from serving this great country and making my family proud.

I had the chance during that time to meet some of the guys that I would create a new bond and a lifetime of memories with. This included someone I'd have to say was the greatest storyteller of all time, a man who would make fun of you straight to your face while everyone else was around, and somehow you felt good after he did. Brett Marihugh was all business and never let me down in any way. He was always there for everyone, no matter what and without fail. He made everyone laugh and always knew how to control a room. He'd been a cop and a Marine, before eventually becoming a SEAL. He blessed everyone that came his way, and always had a way with his words. He also helped me with the second phase dive procedures that we needed to do in order to pass, while I was still rehabbing my shoulder among the Rollbacks.

Brett had been rolled back in second phase for failure at the very dive procedures that he was now teaching me. I jumped in and he walked me through everything. He told me there was no way that this was going to be the reason he wasn't going to be a SEAL. I saw him and Seth Lewis and other Rollbacks doing this every single day for hours on end, until dark most days. After a while, those two could do all the procedures with their eyes closed and faster than everyone else with them open. They were the kind of people that I wanted to be around, positive influences I trusted to no end, possessing exactly the kind of work ethic required to make it through BUD/S and become someone truly special. They both helped me out a lot and I helped them as best I could.

I made the best of my time while I was a Rollback, doing my rehab along with practicing whatever drills and exercises my injury allowed for. That's what I'd learned when I'd spent nearly three years in some combination of crutches and leg braces. The only way to successfully deal with adversity is to make the best of it, to find the silver lining in the clouds. That may be simplistic, but it doesn't make it any less true. In my case, while in Rollback land, that meant both building a stronger relationship with the instructor staff and meeting a ton of guys who imbued in me the reality that the lifestyle of a SEAL was only meant for those with wills strong enough to overcome anything life throws at them. I figured my own experiences gave me a head start but I also came to learn how much

I had to learn. I heard stories, and got to see what things were like outside of training. Being Rollbacks, and having similar hurdles to overcome, provided the same bond I'd enjoyed with my BUD/S classmates prior to tearing up my shoulder.

It was definitely improving, with all the post-surgery rehab. But every time I thought I was over the hump, I'd suffer a setback, usually because I tried to do more than it was ready for me to do. Three months into Rollback, I gave my shoulder its biggest test yet with a drill called Logs. We were enduring a Level 3 beat-down that meant doing two and a half hours of log physical therapy on the beach, as punishment for one of our number messing up somehow. Because of that one guy, we were placed in groups of five or six and had to lift up a telephone pole and do a workout with it together. As we got the call to show up to the beach in five minutes from wherever we were, we knew we were about to get hammered for the mistakes and wrongs done by a single idiot. The thing the instructors were trying to get us to remember was that if one guy makes a mistake, then everybody pays the price. That's the standard, that's the lesson to learn.

It had only been two months since my surgery, though, and my left shoulder couldn't handle the log's weight over my head, so I dropped my left arm and held on only with my right. The last thing I wanted was to return to medical and, luckily, it hurt but was stable in the socket. I iced it, determined to tough things out, and a few days later I was able to get back into the swing of things. On the verge of getting back into training to finish what I had started.

It turned out all of my rehab and hard work in practicing lifesaving maneuvers, as well as swimming with pants and boots on, really paid off. On the first day of the graded evolution lifesaving, the very drill that had banished me to Rollback land months before, my lead instructor called me first, as loud as he could.

"Bisher, get over here! Are you ready to bring it?"

"Hoo-yah!" I cried out, flashing the biggest smile I could, while all the other instructors looked on, their eyes cheering me on.

"Oh yeah, baby!" the lead instructor followed. "Show me what you got!"

I got in the water and crushed that thing. Every instructor I "rescued" gave me a hard struggle and was out of breath by the time we were done. I knew that I earned my spot to make it past that block of training. All my hard work, practice, and self-talk got me through it. I classed back up with the current group in BUD/S class 265, consisting of great warriors who would "cry havoc and let slip the frogs of war," like true leader Brendan Looney, compassionate Kevin Ebbert, the unique and weird stories of Pat Feeks, the life of the party Brett Marihugh, and the monster Seth Lewis. Each person was different and came from varied backgrounds, but we were united by a common theme—a call to defend the freedom that we all felt must be earned, not entitled to.

During second phase training that followed Hell Week, I made it through the grueling pool competition. I didn't have many issues there, because of all the help I'd received from the other Rollbacks. I felt comfortable underwater now and could hold my breath for a long time, so that helped. I made up a dance to the Nelly song "Air Force One" just to remember the right steps to the procedures in the pool comp, including the process of donning SCUBA gear in rapid fashion. It was a big hit with the guys, and they always wanted me to do the dance, especially to lighten the mood after a long, hard day and/or night of training. That song would come on and all eyes would gravitate toward me until I busted those moves. Many guys then followed suit, and these were special moments indeed, made even more special by the camaraderie of not so much brothers-in-arms, but brothers who'd hurt their arms or something else. Brothers bound by the common experience of enduring pain and hardship, while refusing to accept defeat.

The third phase training that followed was actually fun, because I know I'd left the worst behind me, not even the remotest possibility I'd go for that bell at this point. This was the phase that included advanced weapons and explosives training from great instructors who long practiced what they were now preaching. Becoming a SEAL was suddenly very real, my dream on the verge of being realized.

But, at times, I felt empty for some reason. Maybe I was just coming down from an incredibly intense high that had endured for months. Having, at long last, successfully completed BUD/S, I felt myself struggling, racked by doubt and questions of whether I was truly worthy of this mantle. I didn't know it at the time but my soul was engaged in a struggle I'd come to understand far more in later months. At this point, the best way I could articulate the conflict raging inside me was that I'd been feeling as if I'd succeeded in spite of God, instead of because of Him. The numerous setbacks I endured made me want to ask Him, "What do you want from me?"

I was training to give my all to the greatest cause there is: dedicating myself to fighting pure evil. And, given that I was pursuing such a noble endeavor, why wasn't He helping me, instead of impeding me? So at the virtual apex of my life, here I was at a spiritual crossroads.

Then, while on a training mission in the mountains of Alaska, I was leading a group of guys to what we call our "extraction point," the spot where we'd get picked up. We were on our way down from the mountain in the predawn four o'clock hour. Everyone was cold and tired, and ready to get moving through the freezing rain pelting the icy mountain. I had the point, or the job of leading my team to the right location on time, so naturally I was eager to get us there as fast as possible. About halfway down the mountain, though, I checked out an animal path to see if it was safe enough to traverse in order to save time. Just as I was peering over the side of a ledge I'd stepped onto, the earth gave out from under me. I hit my head, then rolled and hit my left shoulder, my fall broken only by the overstuffed backpack I was hauling

The OIC (Officer in Charge) rushed to my aid, yelling, "You okay?"

I grunted an affirmative answer and struggled back to my feet, fearing I'd destroyed my shoulder yet again. "We can't do it this way," I called out to him, realizing that, thankfully, it was still intact. "We need to find a better path."

And, with that response, I realized I'd found my way again, but I was about to face my biggest test, my biggest challenge, yet.

What You Can Learn from This...

1. When you have a boat on your head and you sprint as hard as you can, you find out who will be there for you when it really matters later in life.

2. Setbacks are just comebacks waiting to happen, if you are willing to put in the extremely hard work.

3. If I kept doing things the same way without adapting to what my circumstances lead me to, I would surely fail. I must stop revaluate and then adapt.

CHAPTER 9

The Accident

San Diego, California; November, 2007

The last moment before I jumped, I remembered thinking that we were unusually low, fifteen hundred feet at most. As if the winds had somehow dragged the plane further down. I could see bushes. I could see trees. I could see the leaves blowing in the breeze.

This doesn't seem high enough. I remember thinking to myself, but then I heard the jumpmaster scream, "Go, go, go!"

So I went.

In those final steps before I disengaged from the line and plummeted to the earth, my feet felt like lead boots stomping on the ground. I was air blind in that moment, no idea what to expect because the wind was blowing in my face. After I jumped, I tried very hard to keep my eyes open to gather in everything that I could, with my chin shoved into my chest.

"God, please open this chute!" I yelled out loud, beginning to count in my mind as soon as I jumped from the door.

Jumping from the plane left me feeling like a feather in the wind. I was upside down, watching my feet but seeing the sky beyond them while tumbling through the air, reminding myself to pick up my count from where I started when I first dropped.

One thousand three, one thousand four...

The wind hitting my face felt like a hard slap, maybe even a punch. I could feel the adrenaline surging through me, chilled to the bone even though my blood, literally, seemed hot. I felt a rush surge through me, followed by a tingling sensation accompanied by a flutter in my stomach like the kind that comes when you're looking down from the edge of a cliff.

One thousand five...

That was the point I looked up to see if my parachute had opened, or if I needed to pull the metal handle on my reserve chute. But in that moment the canopy unfolded like a billowing sheet spread over a bed, followed by the shock of the sudden recoil that slowed me some, but not enough, as the ground came up fast.

Just minutes before, I was attached to an anchor line cable on the open side of a ramp-type plane, much smaller than the typical C-130 SEALs use for training, feeling the wind twist and turn me about. It was the kind of day that would keep recreational jumpers home, but Navy SEALs aren't recreational jumpers. A mission is a mission, whether it's a training exercise or the real thing. The elements don't discriminate, and we don't fly back to base because the conditions aren't favorable, not when far worse ones may await our next jump into a war zone. So here I was, at the ripe old age of twenty-three and eighteen months removed from the completion of BUD/S training, continuing to hone my skills.

Today's was a low-altitude jump. We were flying over southern San Diego, an area where the weather is almost invariably fair and clear. On this day, though, the Santa Ana winds were picking up and the clouds were pushing in, the sky dominated by massive gray clouds rolling over the east side of the mountains from the ocean. The air was crisper up there, not like in free fall when you're jumping from 12,000-plus feet. I could smell the fumes of the engine pushing through the open door, the gusty winds quaking the plane harder. All I could hear were my buddies in front and behind me, the mood a bit more tense and anxious now that we'd gotten our two-minute warning. That's when I started pounding the by-the-book procedures of jump training in my head. Make sure that I considered all possible scenarios, so I was ready for anything.

But the book said little about what I was soon to encounter.

I was hooked onto a cable inside the aircraft with a universal static line hook that extended down into my hands. It's literally a lifeline that today was the only thing keeping me inside the plane until my turn came to jump, at which point you realize you're trusting your life to the twenty-nine pounds of canvas that comprised the MC1 series parachute. The light flashed green just as I reached the front of the line, and I dropped into the buffeting crosswinds.

This was called a static line jump where you just fall out of an airplane and the parachute opens at the five-second mark. All you're really doing is controlling the fall, your speed, and direction. Just like paratroopers in World War II, Korea, Vietnam, and so many more. The difference today was the windy conditions that made us wonder if we were even going to jump. And right up to the moment the green light flashed for the first time, I thought we might be on the verge of flying back to base.

Low-altitude drops come with their own unique risks and challenges and no drop is ever routine; it may seem like it was for us because SEALs were always in harm's way, but there's just too much that can go wrong at any time.

And it was about to go wrong for me.

As I dropped toward the canopy formed by the trees, I had to remind myself to breathe, talking myself through the process in the moment my parachute opened fully and I looked back for the toggles, so that I could hold one side to execute a turn to make sure I was going against the wind, instead of with it. You never want to land with the wind because you'll be traveling at a pace too fast for the chute to adequately and safely slow your descent. That's what the book says, but in conditions like this the book gets thrown out.

I'd been able to maintain control for the first thousand feet or so, but things went bad from there. The crosswinds caused a complete shift in direction. See, as you drop to the earth what you're trying to do is go against the air current. That creates a cushion, a buffer to slow the rate of decent. Essentially your drop speed and the wind cancel each other out. That, though, wasn't going to happen once the winds shifted and grew to near gale force. All of a sudden, there was no cushion for me, no buffer. Instead of working to slow my rate of descent, those winds increased it.

The wind blowing into my face made it feel as if I had my head stuck out of a moving car, but I managed to will myself to go through the technical steps to make sure I didn't die on impact. Suddenly the tree line was at eye level and I felt myself bracing for impact, still instinctively cognizant of the fact that my descent was too rapid and I was left completely to the whims of the wind. I had about fifty feet to go before my body hit the ground like a rag doll. I tucked my feet and knees together, the idea being to land on those feet, let the impact roll through your calves and up the rest of your legs before finally reaching your butt, when it's time to roll. You don't want to land with your feet apart because that's a sure recipe for breaking your foot, ankle, leg, or some combination thereof.

On a normal static line jump I would've been fine. But today the crosswinds had changed and I was going with the wind instead of against it. Nothing I could do but brace for impact. The last thirty feet the wind picked up, blowing from my back so hard that my clothes were shaking and driving me forward even faster. The last moments before I hit the ground followed in complete silence. Other than the roar of the wind through my ears, the world had gone quiet.

I landed on a flat stretch of ground that was rock hard, like hitting concrete. Even under the best of conditions, a drop off a static line was equivalent to jumping out of a second-story window and landing on your feet. I should know, since I used to jump off roofs as a kid.

Like I said, I was a kid.

I fought the wind to position my feet as best I could. But when I hit the hard ground, I heard a very loud pop in the hip socket of my left leg where my hip joins the pelvic bone. A burst of searing heat to the area followed, and then my legs felt like someone had ripped them out from beneath me. My head flew forward and I slammed into the ground. I was knocked out briefly, my Protech helmet the only thing that saved my life. I lay there and stripped it off to find a neat crack right down the center. I may have passed out again; I may not have. Time became a blur that made it difficult to be sure of anything, until I heard the four-wheeler coming to my aid.

I looked up at the sky. The world was still spinning and the ringing in my ears just wouldn't let up. I managed to unhook the strap on the side of my shoulder so that I wouldn't get blown away and rolled my parachute into a ball.

"Are you okay, are you okay?" I heard a voice ask through the ringing in my ears.

"I feel fine," I yelled back, my thumb up as high as I could put it, aimed toward the hospital corpsman on the DZ (drop zone) coming to my rescue.

I feel fine.

Sounds simple enough, but the simple phrase has real meaning in the SEAL lexicon. It was what you said during the pipeline in the second phase after you came out of the water on a dive procedure. I said it that way so that my buddies on the ground would get a laugh and assume I was okay.

Even though I wasn't. Far from it. My legs started to shake and the hip socket on which I'd taken the brunt of the impact kept getting hotter. It felt like the socket was on fire, stoking painful memories of a childhood I'd spent a measure of in leg braces thanks to the same hip, something I'd never shared with anyone in my BUD/S class.

Here we go again, I couldn't help thinking.

Uh-uh. No. I wasn't going to allow it. I'd just dropped from fifteen hundred feet out of a perfectly good airplane, and I was going to get up and run it off. So I shrugged off the corpsman's offer of help and climbed back to my feet. The pain was so intense it felt like my blood was boiling. I tried to put weight on that side, only to stumble. Then I ground my teeth, quickly found my composure, and told myself I got this.

At least I hoped I did.

I started to walk it off, but the pain felt like being stabbed over and over again with a sharp blade stuck in my hip. The landing I'd just endured in the drop zone of dusty, uneven ground within view of an airport near the Mexican border was plenty harder than anything I'd ever experienced before. I couldn't just tuck and roll the way I did as a kid jumping off rooftops, not attached to a parachute. I had to do what's called a PLF, or Parachute Landing Fall. That's exactly what happens—you land while falling. But I wasn't in a good spot at all to land and I had no control over my parachute. The crosswinds were so bad that I'd been unable to steer in any direction, so when those winds turned again on me before I landed, I went from traveling at about fifteen miles an hour to thirty or so.

Not good.

Unfortunately, this type of thing happens; it's part of the job. Everyone who's ever jumped knows this, so what happened to me wasn't anybody's fault. Not the people in charge of this operation or my own. It just happens, and sometimes the very same thing happens in combat scenarios too. You jump in all situations to prepare yourself for that day. The risks are there, but you accept them because you need to be ready for any eventuality. And I could take solace in the fact that I could walk, that maybe my hip was just twisted and would show quick improvement.

My next training jump was the day after the hip injury. SEALs are conditioned to deal with pain. Never give up or give in is our ethos, the code we live by. You don't quit in combat and you don't quit in training either, because we train for war and fight to win. So the next day, still racked with pain, I hobbled to the aircraft, favoring my right leg the entire time. But conditions were far better than the day before, and I hoped that would be enough. Jumping, I landed solely on my right leg so that I wouldn't damage my left leg any further than it already was.

After that last jump was over, though, I could barely move my injured leg. That new pain was like none I'd ever felt, and I knew something was terribly wrong. I couldn't even move the leg until I forced it out with a couple pops and some grinding. I hoped again the pain would go away, that time was all I needed, but it only got worse.

Never give in, never give up.

I pushed on for one month and then another. When you're not deployed on a mission, you're training for what comes next. Every day, no exceptions. And I'd been through this before, as a kid when a congenital disorder had ruined my childhood. If I could gut through it then, I could gut through it now.

And that's what I did for nine months, swallowing ibuprofen by the handful and learning to cope, to compensate. It's amazing what your body can endure, and I was still only twenty-five years old. My future, despite the pain with which I'd grown used to living, couldn't have looked brighter. On the personal side of things, I'd just gotten married, in April of 2009, but our honeymoon had to be put off due to my team's training schedule.

Part of that training included toting a fifty-pound rucksack on a mountain climb. I told myself I was going to prove I could manage my injury by finishing in the top five. A big test, for sure. As SEALs we react as well as think and, ultimately, rising to the occasion means falling back on your level of training. That explains why we take it so seriously.

The whole duration of that climb I felt my hip grinding and popping. The pain was tolerable, so I pushed myself some more, working my way through the trail with the top five still in my sights. And I made it to the top right behind my OIC, number two on the list. So maybe, just maybe...

Uh-uh. Nope.

On the way down the mountain, every single step got harder and my leg got more and more difficult to move. I made it down, but over half the troop passed me, and I was done. I couldn't do anything else the rest of the day, could barely move. I sat in an ice bath until I couldn't feel a thing, and then I took the regular ibuprofen that went down like candy.

That became my everyday routine. But as time passed, I only got worse. After everything I'd been through, all the adversity I'd faced that had gotten me to this point, I started to wonder if this was how my military career, and my dream, was going to end. That I'd finally pushed my battered body past its limits and was paying the price at last for so many months of ignoring what was clearly a very serious injury suffered in that parachute accident.

"No way!" I told myself. "No way!"

I was going to continue to try to gut my way through it, envisioning myself as Superman. My wife knew better, knew what I was going through. Nikki, the most exquisite gem in all of the world, the most wonderful, beautiful woman to ever walk the earth. When I was away, every time I closed my eyes I'd see her dark hair, greenish eyes, and flawless skin. Nikki's a combination of Caucasian, Lebanese, and African American, accounting for the uniqueness of her beauty. I was awestruck the first time I laid eyes on her.

My lifelong friend David and I walked into a Best Buy to get a CD. And we both looked at her behind the register and said, "Did you see her?" at exactly the same moment. The whole time we were in the store, we were devising a plan as to what we were going to say when we got to the cash register. As we walked up to her, I calmly smiled and looked her straight in the eyes, feeling my insides melt. And then I said hey, she said hey, and when I bought the CD, I said something like, "Thank you. Have a great day," at which point David flashed me a look.

"Like what are you doing, bro?"

I didn't answer him because I was still tongue-tied.

We casually walked out of the store and as soon as the doors closed he burst out with, "Why didn't you say anything, dawg! You lost it, you ain't got no game no more, you lost it! I dare you to go back in there and get her number!"

"What are we, back in the fifth grade?"

Based on his response, I guess we were. "I'm skipping right over the double dare: I triple dog dare you, boy!"

Before we got to the car, I turned around and said, "Watch me!"

I walked right back into the store and strolled straight to Nikki's register.

"You know," I told her, "my friend dared me to come over here and get your number, but how about I give you mine, and maybe you can give me a call sometime?"

"No," she said, "that's okay."

Talk about deflating! In that moment time stood still, I having just been rejected by the most beautiful woman on the planet. Guess I had to live with it and was already picturing Dave's response. But then Nikki grabbed a discarded sales slip and wrote her name and number on the back.

"Thanks," I told her. "I'll call you later."

And I walked out as smooth as silk. As I approached Dave, once I was certain she couldn't see me, I threw up my hand with the paper in it, did a handspring into a backflip, and then flashed the back of the sales slip to him.

"No way, no way!" Then, without missing a beat, he added, "But does she have a friend for me? Can you check? Come on, man, hook a brotha up!"

The realization I could no longer gut things out came the same month as our wedding. That just didn't seem fair to Nikki, who, to some extent, had lost the man she'd fallen in love with on that very same mountain where my hip had locked up solid and would no longer release. She would wake me up at night because my leg would be shaking uncontrollably, forcing me to get it unstuck out of its locked position. I couldn't stand, sit, move, run, or swim without the hip grinding against my bones. My left leg would lock into a position, creating these waves of pain so intense I could actually hear a high-pitched sound that drowned out the rest of the world.

This began happening with increasing frequency, and I'd have to stop everything and hold my position, just to keep from yelling or losing my cool. The leg would stop moving, seize up all of a sudden, and all I could do was grab it and push my thigh down so that the hip socket would pop and I could at least move again.

"You need to see a doctor," Nikki kept telling me. "This has gone on long enough."

"If I can walk, I can train," I told her, trying to explain my stubbornness in waiting for things to take care of themselves, which they clearly weren't. "I can deploy."

"And what happens when you can't walk anymore?" she asked me. "What if you're doing so much damage to yourself that you end up in a wheelchair for the rest of your life?"

I had no answer. I honestly believed I'd get better, but so far that faith wasn't paying off. The truth was I didn't want anyone to know the severity of the problems I was having and, so far anyway, I was hiding it well enough to avoid the scrutiny of my teammates. Everyone in the unit was dealing with physical issues of their own, and I kept up the charade that mine were no worse than anyone else's. I guess I was embarrassed. I guess I recalled all too well what it felt like to be called a "cripple" as a boy, of not being able to play sports with the other kids, of being sentenced to a life on the sidelines. For me, becoming a Navy SEAL was about overcoming all that, proving to myself that I could do and be anything I set my mind to. Now all that was in jeopardy and I found myself angry at everyone as a result. Angry at myself, my wife, at God.

All He'd put me through, just to have this happen to me...When was enough *enough*? I'd wonder on the worst nights when the pain kept me awake.

One day, my team was out drilling in the desert on a mountainside. We were practicing what's called the "Downed Man Drill," where you're responsible for carrying your buddy to safety no matter how far that might be. It was hot out, over a hundred degrees when we arrived to set up. But the drill didn't take place until dark under night vision, something SEALs are intimately acquainted with. So it was only about seventy-five degrees out with no moon to break the pitch-black sky.

Each step I took felt like I was walking on large stones, or groupings of uneven rocks mixed with dirt. There were hills and valleys and not a single sign of civilization anywhere amid the mountainous terrain. My partner for the drill weighed 230 pounds, and it was time for me to evac his faux wounded form. I lifted him up over my shoulder and started to shuffle. I could feel something shift in my left leg, followed by pain like somebody working a knife around deep inside. He was playing the wounded one, but I was the one who wanted to scream. After two minutes of walking with his weight seeming to push my feet through the ground, I went to take a step up the hill and my leg locked into place. Both of us went down. We got a mouthful of dirt and rock and blood. My hip socket had finally given out and my leg wouldn't move at all. I couldn't get it unstuck this time, as I'd been able to these past ten months. So he picked me up and carried me the rest of the way, the roles of the drill reversed.

For the second time in my life, I felt utterly helpless, a little boy again bearing the taunts and glares of my classmates. I thought I'd finally moved beyond that, my service making up for all the years I'd lost. Now, though, I was right back where I started: nine years old in that hospital bed. Helpless, lame, and without a purpose.

A failure.

A quitter.

Somebody nobody could count on.

I needed to get better. I'd done it before, and now I'd have to do it again. But I hadn't done it alone as a boy and I couldn't do it alone now either.

The day after my collapse in the training exercise, I made my way to the medical center back at base and limped up to the reception desk.

"I need some help," I told the clerk. "I need to see a doctor."

What You Can Learn from This...

1. No matter what plans you have for yourself, something will set you back. Are you going to have a victim's mentality or be someone who will persevere?

2. Sometimes it's better to be smart than hard.

3. There is always someone out there that knows more than you or sees things from a better point of view. Don't ignore that. I had to listen to my wife; she has the gift of wisdom when I need it most.

CHAPTER 10

Fighting Through

San Diego, California; 2009

Our Navy doctors staff was top notch. They were all too used to dealing with people who had gotten blown up, lost limbs, been paralyzed—you name it, this staff has seen it.

A physician specializing in that kind of trauma named Sarah was the first to check me out the day I finally came in for treatment. She was five foot four, 125 pounds maybe, about the same size as my wife, Nikki. She had blonde hair, blue eyes, a cute button nose, and gentle, soft hands that were reassuring on their own. This was the clinic that the Team Guys went to when they're rehabbing their injuries or receiving care for their wounds. Distance wise, it was only about a quarter mile from where my team was on the base at that time, but it felt like an entirely different world boasting a set of priorities entirely different than ours.

"You're in a lot of pain, aren't you?" she said, after taking one look at me.

"Yes, ma'am," I nodded, "I am."

Sarah read through my files, particularly the part about what had happened during my parachuting accident. She wanted me to try some alternate forms of rehab before we considered surgery. So we started a workout session to help me regain my strength and to give Sarah an idea of exactly what I could and couldn't do.

It was obvious I couldn't move my leg without extreme discomfort, and if I tried to put added weight on it, or did anything approaching an athletic motion, it would pop or grind or both. The pain was at its most excruciating during what were supposed to be my therapy sessions with Sarah, the thought being that I'd gradually regain my mobility and, with it, my strength. Stretch out all the accumulated scar tissue, recover my muscle memory and be good to go. Almost as simple as saying take two aspirin and call me in the morning.

Except it didn't turn out that way.

Every day I would go to the clinic for rehab, knowing the pain I was going to have to endure. But it was for the best, a painful means to an end. I knew that Sarah and the rest of the team at the clinic were looking out for me so that I could get back out there and do my job as a SEAL. And if enduring more pain was what it was going to take for me to get better, then so be it.

When I walked into that room to get treatment, I was ready for the pain train. After we were done with our exercises and stretches, Sarah would have me lay down on a bench so she could attach a contraption on me. She'd wrap a grouping of leather straps around my legs to give her the leverage she needed to stretch the part of my hip flexor on the front of my leg where it meets the pelvic area. She'd try to force my leg out of its locked position and create some space, a cushion, so that my bones would stop grinding up against each other.

She tried her hardest, and I was so grateful for the relief these torture sessions seemed to be producing. But that relief never lasted very long at all and was often gone even before it was time for me to leave. As soon as I walked out of that building and sat down or walked around, the pain and the grinding came back in full force. It was pain without purpose. I was accomplishing nothing, achieving nothing.

Having spent a measure of my childhood in comparable pain that stole my dreams, I seemed on the verge of losing my biggest dream at all.

Serving as a Navy SEAL.

I felt no different than the little boy sentenced to life in a bed and then needing crutches under my arms to get anywhere at all. I realized that had become a metaphor for my entire life: going nowhere.

I hated that life. I hated going through all of this pain again. I hated where I was with my therapy and that I had nothing to show for it. I hated the fact that I had let my brothers-in-arms down. I hated that I couldn't prove wrong all those people back home who'd hurled "cripple" taunts at me as a boy.

Because, as it turned out, they were right.

I was so angry every day dealing with the pain and having to struggle just to complete the simplest motions and actions. But I wasn't about to give up everything that I'd worked so hard for just because of this stupid leg that was, once more, holding me back. I took some solace in the fact that I'd proven the naysayers wrong once before. As a kid, getting out of that bed was motivation all by itself. Now I had an even better one: finding a way back to my teammates, and a way back to the fight. SEALs serve this country; that's what we do and that's what I intended to get back to doing.

Even if I could get back to seventy-five percent of what I used to be—I'd settle for that. If I got to the point where I could just move my leg without it locking up, then I could deal with the pain. I didn't care about that anymore; all I wanted was to be side by side with the guys I served with. They were my family, and I hated the fact I couldn't be there for them. More than anything else, that stuck in my mind and wouldn't let go.

I hated the moment I woke up every morning because that's when the pain was the worst, and I felt the most helpless and distant from ever being physically whole again. I lived between medical tests, hoping to find one that would provide the treatment solution I desperately needed. The most recent was an MRA, which is an MRI with a fluid injection so that the pictures that are taken can see in between the joints and the spaces better. I'd gotten my X-rays already, and they'd confirmed my hip was pretty much a mess. But the medical staff wanted to see exactly how bad a mess had been caused by all the bone-on-bone contact, and how we could best clean it up.

The morning of my MRA, I climbed painfully onto the steel table where they would inject me with the fluid and ink to see what they could see. The first tech who tried to get the needle in between the socket and bone failed to get it in the correct position. He tried and failed three more times, before calling in another tech to see if he could do any better. The needle was very long, and every time they stuck it into me, they had to move it through my muscle tissue to try to get to the appropriate spot.

"Hey, man," I said to the latest technician, as fresh pain shot through my hip, "how we doing? I'm in a lot of pain here. Are we close?"

"Almost there," he said, not very convincingly, even though by that time they were using a camera to help guide the process.

"Almost?"

"Almost."

He failed too.

"Okay," I said, raising my voice in frustration, "who's the oldest guy you've got here? Who's got the most experience? That's the person I want doing this, because it's clear to me that the rest of you guys are just whacking at a piñata that happens to be my body."

Then I spotted an old man with just a few hairs left on his head come in. He looked brittle, but had a warmness about him.

Finally, I thought to myself, *someone I can trust.*

He took a look at my X-rays, the video feed, nodding the whole time.

"I'm guessing the pain must be pretty bad," he said, looking at me.

"Awful."

"Then let's see if we can do something about that."

He called a few more residents in to see this "rare type of thing" and pointed out to them what to look for in the films. I counted fifteen people squeezed into the room before it was over. My pain, and its origins, had become a learning experience. Whenever I had my hip examined in any way, the unique nature of my injury seemed to draw everyone like a flock of birds eating bugs in the summer sky.

The older man finally took out his glasses and then slowly eased the needle into my body, looking at the video and then looking down to make sure he had the right angle.

"There," he said finally.

And it was done—after two hours for what was supposed to have taken only fifteen minutes.

The MRA followed without incident and I was in the rehab room every morning at 7:00 a.m. waiting for the results to come in. Day after day passed and nothing. I began to concoct scenarios in my mind where specialists were being consulted all over the world for something no one had ever seen before and had no idea how to treat.

Turned out I wasn't all that far off.

The results were pretty much what I had anticipated, but worse than what the professionals had been expecting. Bone-on-bone contact had completely torn my hip to shreds. All the cartilage was gone in the socket and on the femoral head. An utter mess, in other words, that I'd actually been living with to a lesser degree before the parachute accident accelerated the deterioration process. I could take some solace in the fact that seeking treatment earlier wouldn't have affected my long-term prognosis in any appreciable way; the damage, added to the congenital condition I suffered from as a boy, had already been done.

It felt like a death sentence for my career, my dreams, and my hope of ever getting back to my SEAL brothers. I felt like a ton of bricks hadn't just hit me, they had entombed me. The Navy doctors were going to send me to a specialist, but the process took weeks that felt like years. There was no light at the end of this metaphorical tunnel and no one familiar with my case at the clinic was offering me much hope. I could see defeat in their eyes, sometimes appearing surprised when I kept showing up every day, as if to say, "Why bother?"

I didn't know who to talk to or where to turn. I wanted someone to tell me that I would be able to get through this the way I wanted to, the way I had before. I wanted a doctor to say, "Yes, we will fix you up and you'll be back to normal." But that isn't what happened.

The specialists, doctors, and therapists all agreed: I could either reclassify or leave the Navy entirely. My SEAL career was finished. There was no option of rehabbing or getting surgery done to my hip area; there wasn't even any talk of that. Was I devastated? For sure. But there was no way I was going to back down after all I'd been through to get this far. I had to find another outcome. I needed to search out all my options and choose the one that best conformed with my goal of getting back to duty. That's all I wanted—a chance. I knew sure things were in the past. A chance, any chance, was the best I could hope for.

That left me with only one viable option: hip replacement surgery, deemed the only way I could get back to my team and return to the field. I didn't want to re-rate or get out. I wanted to get back to being as close to normal as I could.

But the doctor was less convinced, believing I was too young for such a radical approach. He wanted to try some other things first, just as Sarah my physical therapist had tried to do to me before. He recommended a new course of treatment and physical therapy along that line.

"I've already gone that route, Doc," I told him.

"I want you to try it this way. What have you got to lose? Nothing, right?"

Compared to everything I'd lose if I left the SEALs, I thought, but simply nodded.

"And if this new approach doesn't work?" I asked him, after a pause.

"Then you're going to need a new hip."

The surgeon explained he couldn't be sure active duty would be an option after hip replacement surgery. Jumping out of airplanes and pushing yourself to the absolute limits of your physical capabilities were hardly recommended for someone with a metal hip. He asked me what my pain level was on a scale of one to ten. I told him a seven. I should have said ten, but pain had been part of my life for so long that I looked at the relative scale of things differently. I'd forgotten what it was like to get up in the morning without intense agony as my wake-up call.

I ended up taking heavy pain medication, while a final protocol and treatment was determined. I'd resisted it before, but now I just wanted the pain to stop. Just take some pills, self-medicating now, and it will go away, providing a transient, fleeting return to what passed for normalcy, if normal was to be defined as not being able to perform the simplest, most basic actions or motions without pain.

Small victories, remember?

But this was no victory at all. My daily routine became wake up to drugs, go in for some rehab. Then stop by to see my SEAL teammates to see if there was anything I could do for them and to remind myself what I really wanted to do which was to get back training and deploying with them. Then more drugs, turning me into a zombie, one of *The Walking Dead*. When I took them, I couldn't feel much except a dull pain, and life was just cloudy. I didn't care what I was doing to my wife or my friends or my family. I wanted the pain to be gone. And the more it was gone, the more I wanted to take the drugs so it wouldn't come back.

This was the lowest point of my life, marked by an addiction that changed who I was, made me bad at everything I did, especially being a husband. My Nikki was the one who had to deal with the guy who came home after it was all over every day, and had to experience the side of me that lashed out. Our marriage became rocky at best. Being a relative newlywed is hard enough on its own, before adding the fact that all I wanted to do when I got home was watch TV and lay down.

We would just sit in front of the television together for hours. I didn't want to talk because I was in so much pain that I would just yell at her. She was a new girl in a new town and a uniquely insular world, who wasn't social and hadn't had time to make friends yet. She wanted us to go out and see the town of San Diego; she wanted to leave the house, and I didn't blame her. I was afraid she thought that she'd made a terrible mistake by marrying me. She couldn't grasp how much pain I was in. To this day, she recalls me walking around with a clenched jaw and a furrowed brow all the time. The charming guy who would suck up the pain and put on a show, the outgoing charismatic guy she'd fallen in love with was gone, and she missed him as much as I did being him.

The gravity of it all hit home one day when we were riding my motorcycle. I've ridden from the time I was a kid, a staple of my life ever since my brother put that bike together for me and I rode it absent the training wheels. On this day we were just cruising down our street when my hip locked up and I drove the front wheel right into the curb, spilling both of us off the bike. We were only going about five miles per hour, but it was still too much and then I struggled to get up. She gazed down at me with a look that said it all, that in that moment she understood I was just a shell of the man she'd fallen in love with and married, only seeming to get worse in spite of all the treatment.

So we'd skipped the honeymoon phase of our marriage and gone straight to the hell phase. I have no idea how Nikki stuck with me through the entire ordeal, becoming the whipping boy for my lashing out in a drug-induced fog. The meds dulled the pain but they didn't bring me any closer to getting back to my dream. They dulled the pain, but not the heartache.

Reality sucks.

How could I return to life as a SEAL now that I'd sloppily strayed so far from that mindset? I was setting a lousy example of what a so-called hero was supposed to be. Going through the motions, while not letting anyone get close to me. Nobody pulled away from me; I drifted apart from everyone. I hated myself and I hated my life. I was losing control and didn't know what to do. If you have ever been addicted to some sort of drug, you understand how it takes a hold of your life and wraps itself around you, like a vine slowly choking the life out of the tree that spawned it. I felt hollowed out and was empty on the inside. The fog of the drugs consumed my day, dulled the pain, and made me want more all at the same time. These drugs were all that was keeping me going, I thought, these were what will bring me back.

Not even close.

In reality they were turning my skin pale and my muscles weak. I was turning into this creature that crawled out of the darkness like Gollum in the *Lord of the Rings* movies. I was not a SEAL. I was not a representation of what a frogman was, the opposite of how I used to be, but I couldn't stop popping pain meds and sleeping pills. I trusted the doctors to take care of me, but when their efforts fell short, I ended up medicating myself into a sloppy, disgusting, unworthy shadow of the warrior I'd dreamed of becoming.

How was I supposed to be this man that everyone wanted me to be, with all of the emotional garbage and physical pain I was carrying? I looked at my choices and found none I could live with. If nothing else, the pain meds allowed me to stay on a treadmill. Not going anywhere. Just stuck in place. I had so much pride that I let that take over my life. I was thinking about myself and my own selfish desires instead of putting my brothers first. Not thinking about the people around me, or what I was doing to them.

That's when I gave up on myself, that's when I hit rock bottom. And maybe that's what I needed to force me to look in a different direction. In my case, that meant toward God.

I'm not talking just about religion here. I'm talking faith, believing in something bigger than yourself. Because I myself had failed. I could no longer expect to find the answers inside me. If they were there, I would've found them already. Since I hadn't, I either had to look elsewhere, in a radically different direction, or cling to the medication-fueled morass into which my life had dissolved.

After years of torture and struggle to be normal, after the loss of close friends and family and years of anger, after medications and failure to succeed or reach my goals, I turned to God for help. If I wanted to get better, or if I wanted my life to change, I knew I needed the help I couldn't get from medicine, physical therapy, or even from my SEAL brothers.

I needed God. And not just God Himself, but the belief that there was a plan for me, in a bigger picture of something greater than everything around me. Because the answers I needed weren't in that world. And if they weren't there, and I couldn't find them inside me, then it stood to reason that only by surrendering to the belief there is something bigger and greater out there would I find hope again.

This wasn't an easy thing for me to do, because I had never surrendered my life, my dreams, my goal, my future, or my desires to anyone at any time, celestial or otherwise. I had always done things my way and if others didn't agree with me, I'd ignore their wisdom or their disbelief and move past them. This was different. I had tried everything to heal, to make my body right and whole. Having failed physically, drugs having become as much a figurative crutch as the literal ones that once allowed me to walk, I had to look elsewhere; inward, toward my soul. If I couldn't heal myself from the outside in, maybe I could heal myself from inside out. It was my soul that had to change, if my body was to as well.

I realized that I was focused on my desires first and that I wasn't living for anyone but myself and what I wanted, the goals I set for myself. I wanted to get back to my SEAL teammates out of loyalty, brotherhood, honor, and obligation. All noble causes, yes, but still about pursuing what was best for *me*. I had placed myself above others, become my own idol. I knew that if I stayed on that same road, I would end up in an even darker place than where I was in that moment. I had built impenetrable walls around myself out of self-pity, despair, disappointment, and self-loathing over my inability to help myself.

So I took a look down a path paved with fate and the conviction that giving myself up to a higher power was the best way to get back to the dream that was about serving and believing in a cause bigger than pain. A simple dirt path headed up a hill to a road of warmth. By choosing that path, I knew there would be trials to come, and I knew the biggest enemy standing in my way was the angry, drug-addicted man who felt so bad for himself, he couldn't feel anything else. That needed to change. I needed to save myself, before I could get back to the business of saving others.

My goals, you see, hadn't really changed. It was the means to achieve them that had changed. There was nothing wrong with the noble cause that had drawn me to the SEALs and led me to overcome so much in making it through BUD/S training before moving on to combat. What was wrong was the attitude I took on, after adversity entered the picture.

No, what happened to me wasn't fair, not after all I'd gone through as a child and had lingering, sometimes mind-numbing pain over the years as a result. But I had stewed in that moral wasteland for too long and God was the only one offering me the way out. Nobody knows who's behind the famous quote, "There are no atheists in foxholes," but I'm betting it was someone who understood desperation.

I opened the Bible at random one day and came to the Book of Job. A few pages later, in 16:6–16, Job's telling us that he has his back against the wall and his enemies have him. It looks as if he's beaten and staring at death in the face. Job sees no goodness in his life. No end to the torment and pain.

I got chills as I read that, because it seemed the words were aimed straight at me.

I know everyone can relate to this in some way or another: a loss in your family, the death of a close friend, or something keeping you from achieving your goals. Maybe you've lost your job, your faith, your hope, the home where you raised your family.

We've all lost something.

Throughout all of his losses and everything that God made him endure, Job remained faithful. Even though he'd come to hate his life, he persevered and endured in service to something bigger than himself. And his faithfulness was rewarded tenfold.

Thanks to Job and my newfound faith, I could suddenly see ahead again, instead of only back or down. I didn't wake up one morning without pain. I wasn't miraculously healed. Even though I'd found an entirely new attitude and reconstituted my soul, my body was still lagging behind and I remained far away from ever serving as a SEAL again.

But now I was ready and equipped to change that. Just like my SEAL brother Marcus Luttrell, whose incredible exploits were chronicled in his book *Lone Survivor*, made into a great movie in which he was played by Mark Wahlberg. With a broken back and legs after a brutal fight with Taliban fighters that left his best friends dead, he could have just given up and died on that mountainside too. Instead he mustered up enough faith and strength to throw a stone in front of him while he was lying on the ground. Then he crawled to the stone, because it was as far as he could go. But after that, he tossed another stone and crawled to that one too, and kept repeating the process until friendlies from a nearby village found him, once he'd made it all the way off the mountain where he could've died.

Marcus didn't say, "I'm going to crawl more than a mile." Instead, he crawled a few feet at a time. He made a choice not to let adversity stop him, to live on for the brothers he had lost—that was his goal and he achieved it. And to this day when he talks about his own faith, what kept him going, he's quick to point out that maybe it was somebody else tossing those stones for him. Well, now I had turned to that same "somebody else."

And I was ready to follow the stones all the way to becoming an active-duty SEAL again.

What You Can Learn from This...

1. Job had a tough life and everything except his life was taken from him. Even when all hope for me seemed lost and I had no way out, something happened to me. I became stronger through adversity.

2. Job called out to his neighbors and told them they couldn't relate. Lots of people are not going to understand many struggles with me and my life; I know that not everyone will. Being tested in my worst of times leads me to the conviction of what needed to change and the wall of pride that needed to be knocked down.

3. Job felt alone and separated from everyone else. When I felt alone and stuck at the bottom, the good news was there was nowhere to go but up. It may take a while but I knew it would get better.

CHAPTER 11

Surrendering to God

San Diego, California; 2009

"It's even worse than we thought," the doctor said, the MRI scans of my hip laid out on the desk before him. "Whatever surgical remedy we choose, you can't be a SEAL anymore."

I'd come into his office to discuss options for surgery, only to hear there weren't really any viable options at all, at least in his mind. The first thing I thought of was another doctor many years before telling me I may never walk again and would definitely never run. Well, I'd proven him wrong and the next thing that crossed my mind was that I would prove this one wrong too.

Then reality set in. I physically couldn't walk the way I wanted to. My wife had been putting on my socks for the last six months because I couldn't. It was taking over two minutes to get out of the car, just to stand up. I was sitting on this bench, thinking to myself, *I don't think I can do this. I can't do this anymore. I'm lost, I'm at the bottom of the barrel, and there's no way I can come back from this.* It had taken so much willpower, so much anger, so much determination, to get me through everything else up until this point that I just didn't think I had anything left.

I was done.

Mentally, physically, and most of all spiritually, I gave up right there while sitting on that bench. I relinquished my pride and, in a crucial point of demarcation, gave myself up to God. Told Him right then and there, "All right, I surrender my life to you; it's no longer mine. And from now on, it's not my will that matters, it's yours. Where I go from here is up to you."

I'd spent a good portion of my life proving people wrong about me. But I was doing it for me, for my own ego, to make them eat crow. I'd set goals for myself that kept me going and kept me working, because of the achievements I wanted to accomplish. It wasn't about serving God, it was about serving myself. And I was so headstrong about doing everything on my own that I was losing touch with my soul in the process.

Sitting on the bench that day, I realized that attitude had taken me as far as it could. I needed a different one if I was going to endure the aftermath of surgery and get back to the business of being a SEAL. The attitude that had gotten me to this point was the same attitude that had come close to ruining my life on numerous occasions. Everything I'd done ended up putting me even further away from where I wanted to be. Setback after setback produced signals I should have heeded, but ignored instead. Exactly like the prodigal son, I took all of my own wisdom and ran away from Him, only to end up broken, shaken, and living inside a spiritual vacuum. I needed a different attitude if I was going to endure the aftermath of another surgery to get back to duty as a SEAL with my teammates, or whatever God's plan was for my life.

In that moment, everything changed. I was no longer wrestling with my will and aspirations for myself, versus God's will and His aspirations for me. In that moment of realization, we created a path together where I could know what He wanted from me and how I could best serve Him. It was all about faith, about the willingness to give myself up to something greater, so I might become something greater, too, in the process. And the means for achieving that was where the true blessing laid, not with the ends.

I broke the news to Nikki and my family back home. No, I didn't tell my wife that I was struggling to be the man she wanted, or needed. I never wanted her to think that I was struggling emotionally. This was a great void in our relationship. My stoic outlook and actions were what I thought she needed for strength and support. So I resolved to be unbreakable, never showing how vulnerable I often felt.

I asked the church and my close relatives to pray for me as I was going through a very hard time in the military. I felt those prayers because everything fell into place, like nothing I had ever experienced before. Both Nikki and I were seeking a church to call home, and during my struggles to walk around before my surgery we found a rock solid place to rebuild our faith in the form of the Eastlake Community Church. See, things for me just didn't, *poof!*, change on a dime, and life was suddenly great and without concern again. It was a process.

And that process began, to a great extent, when I decided to seek the wisdom of Solomon. To me, he was the wisest man ever to walk the earth, and his story provided both hope and solace. God gave him everything and he lost it all. He disobeyed God in every way, so God informed him that all he'd done in his life, all his vast accomplishments and achievements, would be lost to history, rendered moot in the great scheme of things. The wisest man to ever walk the earth refused to surrender to God's will, and paid dearly when God ripped it all away from him.

And yet his final advice to his fellow man was to "follow the Lord's commands." Seriously? That was the best advice the great Solomon could give me? Well, if it was good enough for him...

Those four words amounted to the new life plan I'd accepted for myself. I now believed that if I followed God and believed in Him, He would continue guiding me down the path He'd already laid out. I think a lot of the time, God was testing Solomon. I wasn't Solomon, not even close obviously, but I do believe He was testing me too. Maybe He wanted to know how much I could take, how much before I'd quit. He was pushing me to my absolute limits and, where I had once resented Him for that, I now embraced the challenge He'd set before me with the certainty that I could be a Navy SEAL again. Just like I had learned to walk, and then run, again.

Of course, maybe in the grand scheme of things, He wanted me to quit, to ring the bell on this phase of my life. But I didn't believe that, not after all He'd put me through to get me as far as I had come. Nope.

See, God wasn't just testing Solomon, as so many believe. God had given him certain commands to obey, yet even though Solomon was the wisest man in the land he still fell short of God's wisdom and understanding of life. He was disobedient, just as I was. He put his will before the Father's, just like me. He was so stubborn to the end of his life. I didn't want to have that happen to me. I realized that Solomon was given wisdom beyond any other man, but he failed because he relied solely on himself, only to see in the end that he should have embraced the help and will of others to help him realize his goals and ambitions.

And God wasn't merely testing me either. He wanted to see what I was made of and if His faith in me was justified. Did I still have the dedication it took to be able to achieve what too many said was impossible? Not alone I couldn't, and I think that was the primary message God was sending me. By opening myself up to Him, I'd be opening myself up to a whole new world I had glimpsed during BUD/S training and then later as a Rollback. I was done slipping back into the selfish mindset I detested from my youth. I needed to banish that part of me from my psyche, from my very being, so I wouldn't feel as if I were being constantly tested.

God, as it turned out, was still on my side.

I underwent hip replacement surgery a few months later, not a single doctor involved believing I had any chance to return to active duty as a SEAL. After the surgery was over, the doctor came in and told me out of all the hips he had done, in all the years, mine was the worst he'd ever seen.

"You must've been in pain for a long, long time," he said.

"Since I was a boy," I told him.

"And you still became a SEAL?" he asked, shaking his head in disbelief. "You inspire me to be a better doctor!"

"I'm still a SEAL. And I'm going to serve as one. Tell me that's possible."

The doctor didn't look like he really wanted to do that. "I don't want to get your hopes up."

"You're not. Just tell me it's possible."

"It's possible. But for someone with your condition, I don't recommend this because you have a higher chance to reinjure or ruin the prosthetic completely. Guys get replacements but they change career paths. I do know that a few other SEALs have had replacements, but they are no longer kicking in doors. They are much older, not twenty-seven, so to my knowledge, it's never been done before in the way you are asking."

"There's a first time for everything, Doctor."

He told me not to do the things he almost surely knew I was going to do anyway, and then said "Good luck," with a slight smile that was either dismissive or hopeful—I couldn't tell which.

I couldn't wait to start physical therapy, since how well I progressed would ultimately determine my fitness to serve as a SEAL. But I wasn't worried, because I had put my faith and trust in God. So the physical therapist and I got started with some rudimentary stretching and strengthening exercises. The worst part of PT was when another guy in the office would use a butter knife to scrape at the scar that had formed over my incision. The idea was too shave back as much of the scar tissue as possible, so it wouldn't hurt when I walked. But, man, did it hurt when he scraped!

And it didn't exactly tickle when I had to get in the arc trainer, which is a treadmill that helps you run, utilizing a limited percentage of gravity so that you're not doing any damage to the already stressed muscles, while still strengthening the muscles and retraining them to do what they used to. I'd rotate using ice and heat on the hip for treatment, and even learned to tolerate sitting in an ice bath. Working the hip free and loose in the pool while swimming proved a great barometer for the progress I was making, and being in the water, doing laps on my own, made for the perfect opportunity to commune with God. That's when I felt closest to Him, when His word rang loudest in my ear through the deafening silence of pulling myself through the water.

I pushed myself every day, taking my rehabilitation as far as I could, while always cognizant of the need to avoid any setbacks from overdoing it. Disciplining myself to hold back a bit was the hardest thing of all, because as I started to make real progress, my thoughts turned to the fact that I was doing this for my guys, my SEAL brothers, for my family, and for our country. That's a very high bar, and before God and I became partners in the effort, I might well have gone too far in an attempt to achieve too much. But I was a different person now, a different person as soon as I awoke from surgery with the realization that my future was all in our hands now: mine and God's. The challenge of something as simple as getting out of bed was nothing new for me, given that I'd been through it twenty years before. I knew what it was like to lose the ability to do the simplest of things, perform the simplest of acts. Where even getting from the bed, or couch, to the bathroom was a monumental challenge. And it was a challenge made doubly difficult this time by the fact that my hip was so deformed to begin with, it took everything the surgeons had to even fit me with a new one. But I had a partner in those efforts now.

Even with that partner watching over me, I was told not to start running until twelve months after I was out of surgery. That gave me the opportunity to work other parts of my body and, more importantly, my mind. Just because I wasn't ready to formally return to duty yet didn't mean I couldn't become versed in something that would help me serve my team once I got back. So I decided to study Arabic and enrolled in a few classes at schools close to the base.

I really wanted to learn Arabic to the point where I could speak it fluently, like a native language. That could make me a great resource and even better teammate, the ideal way to contribute to my team once we were deployed. It was all about bettering myself, taking advantage of the opportunity provided by the limitations placed on my body that in no way reflected any having been placed on my mind. Every time I wanted to slack off for a time, to sit and do nothing, I found another means to better myself and better prepare for my return to the team to ensure that I'd be an asset and not a liability. Studying day and night to become as expert with Arabic as I possibly could allowed me, eventually, to serve as the primary linguist with my team once we were deployed in Iraq. The first step to understanding a culture was understanding the language, and for our part, that would prove to be an invaluable resource. It's not something you necessarily think of when viewing the SEALs as a rapid engagement force, but that was only part of our mission in Iraq.

Thanks to this, and the extensive and grueling rehabilitation I'd undergone, I returned to the teams with a completely different mindset. I wasn't angry and I wasn't out to prove anybody wrong, as I had been in the past. I didn't need to prove anything to anyone other than my new partner, God. I'd found my purpose within His plan, and He repaid me tenfold by guiding my recovery and return to duty. The proof, as they say, is in the pudding and I'm here to tell you that, no matter how much it may seem to the contrary, you are never alone.

I believe God let me fall as often as I did so that I could be stronger after I picked myself up. That's a great lesson, but one that can't be preached; it has to be experienced, and so many miss out because they, like me, lash out at those who don't agree with or oppose them. I never realized how lost I was, until I was found. You probably know exactly what I'm talking about from your own experiences. And I want you to know, too, that if you're struggling with a pain both dark and deep, that it's okay to let it go and let God take over. Following His will and His way doesn't so much represent usurping yourself as expanding yourself. Widening the horizons so more of the world, figuratively and literally, is at your disposal.

Today, I'm blessed to be alive after serving my country overseas in a combat-riddled environment, blessed to be a warrior who walked amongst the enemy with a giant sword. I'm blessed to have experienced so much pain as a child, to have struggled managing a task as simple as getting out of bed or merely walking.

While these experiences didn't appear as blessings originally, in retrospect they helped fashion me into the man I am today, the sum total of all my experiences adding up to a contentment and calm that helped me accept them for exactly what they were: stepping-stones climbing toward a broader and greater place in God's grand view. For me, it comes down to serving God instead of serving yourself. And yet serving Him is the best way to serve yourself.

It's not easy to ask anyone for help, much less to ask God. It takes a certain kind of courage to admit you can't get to the finish line on your own and need someone to drag, carry, or at least show you the way. An apt metaphor for the basis of my relationship with Him that came to define the next phase of my life when the time came to deploy. I have incredible respect for the doctors who made me physically whole again, but they did so with the belief that they could get me walking, but not running; swimming in a pool, but not in the ocean; preparing me for the next phase of my life, instead of the next phase of my life as a SEAL. As much as I'm grateful to those doctors and surgeons, I didn't listen to them when it came to my long-term prognosis.

I listened to God instead.

And he didn't steer me wrong. Instead, he steered me back to the SEALs and my team. I may not have been the fastest guy or the strongest guy, but I knew I could still contribute and be an asset to my team instead of a liability. As I worked on my fitness and on my way back to the platoon, I noticed that I wasn't as strong, and I wasn't as fast. I was limited. I had a grueling time getting back into shape. I was a long way from where I should be as an operator. So I thought about the "boys" and what was expected of me.

The fact that I was told not to run for at least twelve months was not going to happen. Instead, I started in the soft sand on the berms of the beach after only four months. I swam in the ocean with fins twice a week. I studied Arabic for countless hours, asking myself at every turn: When doing anything, how could I do this better, how could I improve? How can I be of use? The most challenging part about training to get back to where you were is acknowledging you're older and more broken than you were back then. To get ready to climb that mountain you thought you had already conquered, only to see that once you climbed that mountain, ten more loom in your way.

I needed to get there, but the fact remained that my body was not the same. I had to once again ignore the negative circumstances that surrounded me and push past the limits imposed on me by others. I did not surrender to the limitations imposed by the words of another man. Instead, I used as motivation the most powerful impetus of all, that being a return to the brotherhood I loved and had cast my lot with.

My family aside, those guys were all I cared about. They were all that mattered. A group of guys who deserved the best I could give them, which is exactly what I intended to deliver. It wasn't about me, or what I had to prove. It was about doing my part to help my team make it through and make it back home safe. Deployment in a war zone means facing life and death every minute of every day. We can't afford mistakes and don't get any do-overs. There are no mulligans in a shooting war.

I don't think men like this get enough gratitude for the things they do. I never quite understood how we could obsess over the Kardashians or a football, basketball, or baseball star for weeks, or about how much a film star made at the box office, and which politician told the biggest lie. Compared to the people who serve our country to preserve the freedom we all hold so dear, all that is immeasurably unimportant. True heroes have no agenda, other than to preserve and protect inherently American values in places that have never heard of the Kardashians. They do what they do so Americans can continue to live their everyday lives without fear of terror in our streets and our towns. They stare evil in the face and say, "I am not afraid! You will not defeat me."

And I was about to rejoin them on the battlefield.

What You Can Learn from This...

1. Walking alone is so hard to do, no matter who you are. We all need the help of others.

2. When I gave up on myself and felt like a failure, God gave me a new beginning that was perfect.

3. In life, you're either in pursuit of greatness or you're regressing. Now is the time to grind.

4. Do not surrender to the will of another man, but only to God the Father.

CHAPTER 12

Fit to Serve

Southern Iraq, 2011

I was deemed "fit for full duty," according the Navy doctors, meaning I could resume all of my "normal" activities. I still went to physical therapy three times a week and worked at getting back to full strength, but I finally made it out of the hole and back into the teams. I was no longer with the team I started with, but I ended up being in the same platoon as my old friend Gotez, the very guy who helped me through the first part of BUD/S training, along with a few others I had a long-lasting relationship with. It was a crazy coincidence, or maybe/probably another way God was looking out for me. The team said they needed an Arabic Level 2 speaker, and that I was the guy that was recommended to them who could fill the slot.

As I reflect on this now, I see that I had to do the things that no one else wanted to do to get to where I needed to be. Isn't it crazy how it all worked out that way?

I then was sent to another language school to help out my platoon's needs so that I could be used in the best way possible. I wanted to be on my A-game leading up to deployment. I wanted my new platoon to believe in me and place their faith in my skills. Just as any person wants to be a positive part of the team and to feel valued and validated, I wanted to do my part.

I looked to Gotez for what to do next and listened to his words, just as I had done a few years before. He was a seasoned vet, along with the rest of the guys. They had all been downrange before, and had amassed more knowledge in that period than others do in a lifetime. So listening to them was always the right thing to do.

After a few more months I was packing my bags, sending my wife and family back home, and preparing for a long-time separation. I didn't see my family for nine months. That puts an extreme stress on any relationship, and it's very hard on everyone.

While I was on deployment, my father called Nikki and told her that a helicopter went down, and asked if I was okay. I hadn't talked to her in a few days, and she was terrified. She didn't have to be in the dark on the situation, but we didn't set up the right communications for her leading to my departure.

On August 6, 2011, thirty-eight people lost their lives in the crash, along with a working dog. Most of those men were SEALs and all of them brothers-in-arms. The CH-47 Chinook was hit by an RPG and everyone died. I mourn the loss of my brothers, but we all know the dangers of the job, and still go.

Nikki could have taken advantage of the Navy's resources to help her along, but she was disconnected from that and was on a kind of emotional island, dealing with my lengthy deployment. She had a six-month-old infant, no day care, no job, and living with our families in their homes rather than her own. She felt outright disconnected, and for good reason.

As for me, it took a solid day's travel to reach the war zone. I was glad to get off the giant plane riding with the huge pallets full of our gear. Flying overhead, I could see the sandy desert land, surrounded by the Iraqi cities in which we'd be operating. I could feel the heat rise as we were descending onto the airfield. I couldn't help but notice the smell that reminded me of something left in the oven for too long, a burnt odor as if the air itself had been singed. That, coupled with the heat, made the hair on my neck stand up, as the sun beat down on us and sweat began to soak through my clothes.

The surrounding colors engulfed our very existence. The hot air could cook an egg if you put it on a rock. Temperatures exceeding 120 degrees on a daily basis were the norm, as was waking up in a pool of salty sweat. Our platoon had the luxury of having a roof over our heads, which was great. At least we had a place to stay and, since the initial push into the Middle East, our base had been outfitted with the basic defenses required to withstand at least minor attacks. Our food was provided by local friendlies; not bad, but it left me missing the pizza and hamburgers I was craving so much. Our platoon struck gold, however, when we found a small galley in our camp that allowed us to improvise a bit and get real creative. It wasn't great food, but given the circumstances, it was amazing to have.

All that was not of my concern, however. For all of us, it was about the mission objective to help out our country and meet the needs of what our orders were. Since I knew the language, I was put in charge of our interpreters and scheduled to meet with the local forces to help them in diplomatic and military objectives. I'm not at all suggesting that I was in charge of this operation, but I was a part of the cadre that was, and I was able to use the skills I'd been taught to assist my platoon in the right way. It was an honor to be a part of the team, to work side by side with heroes. I helped my OIC (Officer in Charge) with key leader engagements and setting things up for operational readiness.

Everyone wants to know everything I did, how I did it, and who I did it with. The complete blow-by-blow. A tell-all account of anything and everything that I saw overseas. There have been several books written by my SEAL brothers about the killing of Osama bin Laden, along with a whole bunch more covering other aspects of our engagements in Iraq and Afghanistan, and I have no intention of commenting on them or trying to emulate their approach. This isn't a book about glorifying my service. Serving with my SEAL brethren forged the greatest bond I could have ever imagined. And, in that service, I was privileged enough to do things the vast majority of people only dream of. Becoming a SEAL was the ultimate challenge for me, and I made it—just barely, but I did.

I was just a small part of a huge operation, and even more than that, I was a newer guy, not an old salty frog who knew everything and everyone. I was a sponge hoping that any of my work would be value added. Praying that God would protect all of my teammates as we did our part to rid the world of murderous, power-hungry people terrorizing the innocent for no other reason than they could.

I was learning on the fly and struggling to keep up. I didn't win the Silver Star or the Medal of Honor, the kinds of awards presidents pin on chests; I can't even name for you the awards I did receive because I didn't feel I needed to be rewarded for doing what I was supposed to do. I did my job, just like we all did. I did it for God and country, in service to both to make both equally proud.

The prologue of this book detailed us getting called to action when an Army Special Forces A Team was under pursuit by hostiles on the road leading into a major Iraqi city. Turned out they were able to lose their pursuers without firing a single shot. But that didn't make the soldiers any less grateful when we rendezvoused with them.

"Yeah! Navy SEALs are my heroes!" one of them yelled at us.

The fact is we may not have been needed at that particular point, but he still wanted to thank us for coming to his rescue at a moment's notice. All in all, a non-incident.

But many didn't go down like that at all.

One night when my platoon was on our way out to our target, I almost lost my life along with everyone else in the Humvee. We had prepped for the mission the same way we always did, and had done our checklist on our team gear, our buddy's gear, and our personal gear, along with making sure the vehicles were prepped, gassed up, and capable of radioing back and forth with a good communications check.

Everyone knew the mission objective, and we were pumped up and ready to get on target. We piled into the Humvee and headed out into the night. It was pitch black, no moon or stars. It was silent, and nothing but the low hum of the big tires gripping the concrete on the road could be heard.

I was again up top manning the mounted .50-cal. in the turret looking for any movement that would raise suspicion, or give me a reason to engage. Since we were the lead vehicle speeding toward the target, I was looking from my nine o'clock all the way over to my three o'clock, scanning the entire scene just as I'd been taught, nothing out there catching my eye as suspicious or dangerous at all.

We were headed north on a paved road when the sand began to hit me in the face. It was a little harder to see, but nothing dramatic.

"Can you see okay?" I yelled down to the driver.

"Yeah, I'm good," he said back.

I continued to scan the road and any objects I could make out, in the distance as well as closer up. As I looked off to my right, I noticed the roadside was beginning to drop off substantially. I looked through the windy sandstorm ahead of us and spotted a bridge and water below off to the right, down about forty feet. Then my eyes moved directly to the entrance to the bridge. Something up there didn't feel right, and I thought I glimpsed a blip in the darkness, like something projected against the scene I couldn't quite make out.

"Barricade!" I yelled as loud as I could, when I finally distinguished what lay directly before us.

We were less than a second from smashing into a cement wall at a local checkpoint going fifty-five miles per hour. Right on cue the driver, Vedy, swung into the hardest right turn you could make in an up-armored Humvee. He turned at a virtual ninety-degree angle and then tried to swerve back to the left so we wouldn't hit the guardrails that extended out from the bridge blocked by all that concrete. The vehicle lifted up on two wheels, and Vedy twisted the wheel back the other way to plant us back on all four. I was still up top in the turret, able to peer over the side off the edge of the road, just before the riverbank and hill met the guardrails to the bridge.

In that moment I had to make my choice of either jumping out to keep from getting squashed between the railing and the vehicle, or trying to hold my ground. But in the next moment the Humvee slammed back to the ground, bounced, and then settled. My head smashed on the top of the turret, and I was immediately grabbed by Manny, my LPO, and Doc, who had his arms wrapped around my legs so I wouldn't fall out of the turret from the inertia of the hit.

Vedy rapidly course-corrected and we were back cruising in the dead of night through the middle of the sandstorm, squeezing past the concrete barrier we'd nearly crashed into to cross the bridge. I got my bell rung pretty bad but I was okay. Inside the Humvee, the rest of the guys made sure everybody was good to go and began to settle back in for the objective. I perched back into position and began my duties once again.

We headed down the road, twenty minutes later off to a dirt road, and then to our rally point. My team conducted a solid mission and we ended up with two hostiles in our possession. Made it back to camp that night without a single casualty, save for my headache.

Mission success.

And no recriminations followed. Not for the spotty intelligence that had failed to identify the presence of a barricade along our route. Not for the driver, who I'd known my entire career in the Navy, for not spotting it in time to avoid the drastic response he was forced to engage. We do our jobs, always expecting the unexpected to occur, and never pointing fingers when things don't go off exactly as planned. We're trained to respond to each moment unfolding into the next. A warrior's mentality postulates that you always keep pushing forward no matter what, without making excuses.

Nothing could account for the zero visibility we drove into, and Vedy's quick actions had saved my life and everyone's in the vehicle. I didn't think about it at all after the fact. I didn't let it cloud my judgment for the rest of the night, and no one else did either. Those are the type of guys I wanted to my left and to my right. Warriors whose pursuit of mission success is clear and direct.

It wasn't until after we got back and were eating dinner/ breakfast that I went up to Vedy and told him how close I'd been to jumping. I now have a "one-up" story to tell and can always bring it up whenever we're around to give him a hard time. And I *do*! It usually goes like this:

"Hey Vedy, what up, bro!? Remember when you almost killed me? Ha-ha! That was fun!"

I was able to pick up cultural and linguistic skills from the Iraqi interpreter team members who were either born in America or fled there at some point. They wanted so much to serve honorably, because this was their homeland and they understood the cause. They gave me the key phrases to look for and the correct way to be culturally savvy with the locals, when we'd enter their neighborhood or talk with them in their homes. The Iraqi interpreters were there for us every step of the way. They went on patrol, fought by our sides, because they wanted their countrymen to be free of the oppression that had chased them out of the country and had now chased them back.

I spent countless hours with the locals, getting to know what motivated them and how to look for a tactical edge or see life through their eyes. What I learned through all of this is that, like us, they want to feel safe and freed from a radical Islamic mindset of convert or die. They wanted help to be able to live without the fear of being dominated and ruled by people with a power-hungry desire to make others bend a knee to their ideals.

Being able to understand that part of the culture aids the entire team, by helping to build a rapport with the Iraqis. The same applies for any nation or business. I learned that the Iraqi soldiers were not a bunch of savages, one of the many misconceptions about their country. Many of them pulled out their phones to show me pictures of their families, or photos of their kids in their wallets. Some of them were even trying to find a way to America to get out of the war-torn life they were in.

The people of that area may have loved or hated us depending on their political views, but at the heart of it they all wanted the same thing. They wanted peace for their homeland, or at the bare minimum, security for their families without being radicalized by the local thuggish leadership. I could see the hope blooming in their eyes the more we worked together. You could tell that they had a dream, and that they believed in our capacity to help them realize it. These Iraqi soldiers clung to the culture in which they'd grown up, a culture that barely resembled the depths to which their country had sunk. In a word, these brave men wanted what we all want:

Freedom.

The freedom to dream, to believe in something better, to not be ruled by a man who believes he is God or his own idol. Just like the author of the book *Code Name Johnny Walker* (William Morrow; 2014 edition) who was the only Iraqi native interpreter who had real experience dealing with matters top secret and above. The book is subtitled, *The Extraordinary Story of the Iraqi Who Risked Everything to Fight with the U.S. Navy SEALs,* for good reason. The man we knew as Johnny Walker was a great operator, as well as interpreter, and his heroic efforts saved the lives of countless American forces, not just SEALs, providing immeasurable help in our fight against pure evil. It was people like him that proved to us this place was worth fighting for, that it was worth protecting from those who wanted to do it harm.

Living in a war-torn state for your whole life is, to say the least, difficult for Americans to relate to. You cannot really relate to it at all, unless you've been there and experienced it firsthand. Being able to listen, speak, and help others in need was a blessing and an incredible challenge and responsibility to try and wrap my head around, but I did, and it was a true honor to serve my country in that way.

Laughter makes the experience more tolerable. It helps keep us grounded and bonded. But there are tears to be shed for those heroes not as lucky as I was. I mentioned their names before, but they bear repeating:

Brendan Looney, Pat Feeks, and Kevin Ebbert.

Since I wrote in the prologue that I think about them every day, many more days have passed and not one has gone by without me continuing to think about them, all the time knowing that they gave their lives for something they believed in, something bigger than themselves. True service begins with that realization. And I feel, to a great extent, that writing a book that seeks to glorify, even embellish, the actions a warrior takes is an affront to men like Brendan, Pat, and Kevin, who never got a chance to do so. The last thing on their minds was using their experiences to climb the bestseller lists. They were thinking about families they'd left behind, the report cards they couldn't sign, and the shopping lists they couldn't fill at the supermarket.

I never wanted to write a book, to let people into my personal life or to share my struggles with the world. I didn't feel comfortable with it, didn't want anyone to think, especially among my brothers, that I was exploiting or monetizing my experience.

So why am I doing it now?

Because I know that there are people out there, like me, who have difficult, if not impossible, hurdles to overcome, and who've maybe lost hope, just as I did for brief periods of time. Like sand slipping through my fingers, my life just couldn't be grasped, and others feel that way too. They've lost track of the way forward and feel lost, finding themselves searching for a guidepost, something familiar and comforting to set them on the right path toward fulfillment and happiness.

So I'm writing this book for them, so they can hear it from someone who's been there and found his way through and out. That's why I write, that's why I speak, because I want you to believe that you have something more in you too. If you don't like the way you feel about yourself, you don't have to accept that. Hopelessness is one of the worst feelings on earth; I know because I've felt that way so often in my life. In my case, finding my faith and finding God became the guideposts out of my morass and the catalyst to take me to a place no one believed I could go. But first I *believed*, and that's where it has to start for you too. I found my place, found my purpose, and everything in my life changed. I wasn't just living, I was thriving.

I started to think about this a lot in Iraq, when I found myself revisiting the path I had taken that brought me there. And once my active service ended, another kind of service began that I take just as much to heart, another mission that was equally important, if not even more so.

What You Can Learn from This...

1. You must surrender your life to Jesus in order to save it from a lifetime of battles that end without fulfillment.

2. You have to surrender yourself to your team and the ones around you in order to truly find who you are and be the best that you can become.

3. If you are "all in" your personal desires fade, humility shines, and life is worth all the pain from the past. Teaching others this becomes pure, and you can find peace.

THE ADULT

CHAPTER 13

Lessons Learned

Michigan, Present Day

Today, I spend a great deal of my time mentoring people: primarily professional sports teams, future special operators, and, especially SEAL candidates in the upper Midwest. The question I ask them to a man is, *What are you going to do today to be better than yesterday?* I tell them to work on getting 1 percent better than they were yesterday. Something they can feasibly achieve without having a daunting feeling that the goal is out of reach. And there are lessons I impart on them right from the start, lessons drawn from my own experience:

- ▸ Make sure you do it right the first time.
- ▸ Don't cut corners and don't sell yourself short.
- ▸ You practice how you play and you play how you practice.
- ▸ The moment you think you have arrived, someone else will prove you otherwise and that's how it is.

I have helped mentor numerous teams, as well as many future NSW (Naval Special Warfare) and NSO (Naval Special Operations) candidates, because my service didn't end in Iraq—it had only just begun. With my service in active duty finished, I was left with all the experiences and lessons accumulated over the years in overcoming all the adversity that I'd faced. For me, the realizations that had stemmed from all that, like how bringing God into my life had finally gotten me over the hump, had so recently dawned upon me that I couldn't just walk away and start up a new life. I wanted to share all I had learned with others who'd either lost their way or hadn't quite found it yet, both in and out of the military.

Looking back on what life has thrown at me, and the choices I made, I'd never have achieved anything close to what I was able to do without the help and guidance of others. I think it was English poet John Donne who wrote that "no man is an island," something extraordinarily true in my case. From my family, to my SEAL teammates, to the doctors, to the BUD/S instructors who stood by me every step of the way, to my fellow Rollbacks after I was hurt, I always had someone in my corner and, in my darkest, most hopeless times, I found God holding the stool. I'd already proven to myself that anything was possible.

Now I wanted to prove it to others.

Adversity is defined as a "situation of unfavorable fortune or fate or circumstance" and a "condition marked by misfortune, calamity, or distress." Well, I guess that describes the evolution of my life pretty accurately. Overcoming adversity is more than just a conscious decision—that's only where it starts. You can wake up one morning and decide you want to build a house, but you still need the tools to do it. In the course of my experiences I had found those tools, and now I want to show others facing adversity how to use them.

It begins with ignoring the odds and however much the deck is stacked against you. It begins with you becoming the CEO of your own life, taking it over and not letting other people or circumstances dictate otherwise. There's no shame in failing; the shame lies in quitting because you don't feel up to the task. You think the adversity you're facing forms an impenetrable wall you can't shoulder your way through. That's what happened to me, and in my case, metaphorically, I climbed behind the wheel of a bulldozer and plowed my way straight through that wall.

Want to borrow the keys? Here, take them.

The gas fueling the engine, though, is your belief in yourself. That's where it starts. Before you can realize your dream, you have to believe. The sense of succeeding after repeated failures is far more inspiring and potent than succeeding right out of the box. The more failures, the higher the wall becomes, which will make it all the more enriching when you charge your way through it. The only thing that held me back from what I wanted to do was myself. And as soon as I realized that, I became a party to my own success, instead of an impediment to it. My thoughts and my belief in myself became who I was. Being able to say, "I believe," can take you to a place where you can dream, and then make your dream a reality.

I was headstrong and stubborn in high school, but I never stopped believing in myself, and that fueled my dream to become a Navy SEAL. Believing in yourself is the catalyst for both setting your goals and achieving them. It's not ego, or even confidence really. It's something that springs from your very core as a human being. In high school, I really didn't like who I was, something that dawned on me in the wake of wishing my basketball coach would die. But that didn't make me believe in myself less; it only channeled all that energy in the direction of making myself a better person.

In the weeks and months that followed, I failed every single day. And every single day I'd tell myself to get back up, try again, start over, do it a different way—whatever it took to succeed. Believing in yourself is the key to not watching life pass you by.

"As soon as you trust yourself," Johann Wolfgang von Goethe once said, "you will know how to live."

"You cannot be lonely if you like the person you're alone with," adds the late motivational speaker Wayne Dyer.

No less an accomplished genius than the painter Vincent van Gogh wrote, "If you hear a voice within you say, 'You cannot paint,' then by all means paint, and the voice will be silenced."

And finally, from the scholar Williams Jennings Bryan, no stranger to failure himself: "The way to develop self-confidence is to do the thing you fear and get a record of successful experiences behind you."

I found those quotes in the course of writing this book and was struck by the extent to which each applied to my own life experiences. Believing in yourself is the surest route to success, just as not believing in yourself is the surest route to failure. I'm not saying there are shortcuts, but there is a road map, and it starts with you knowing where you want to go, even if you're not sure exactly how to get there. Alternatively, I'd never want to be like that former high school football star who talks about his glory days on the field from twenty years before. I would never let something like that define me as no more than who I am or who I used to be.

Ryan Williams, SEAL veteran and entrepreneurial success, is a great example of how to keep pushing forward to your dreams by not looking back on what you have done in the past. Even building a very successful apparel company wasn't enough for him. He wanted more, wanted to take what he'd learned during his years of service and apply those lessons to civilian life. So he sold his share of his first company and founded Industry Threadworks to enable him to help others build their brands as successfully as he built his.

"I was a Navy SEAL for ten years which, like a number of other professions, seems like a really cool job, and it is," Williams recently told Maveriqs Academy in, what for me, was an eye-opening interview. "However, at a certain point it becomes 'work' just like any other job. I wanted to branch out and do something different. I wanted to squeeze all of the experiences I could from life, and for that I needed money. I knew I was never going to get rich in the Teams. It was a great experience. I learned a lot about the world and myself, but at the end of the day money is freedom to me, and I wanted to have more freedom in my life. I was roommates with another Team Guy, and buddy of mine at the time. After many nights of thinking and talking about the future we decided that we were going to start a business together. We came up with a dozen different business plans. Everything from party planners to the normal tactical types of things that Team Guys do when they get out. The very last thing we thought of was an apparel brand.

"We started the clothing company knowing nothing about the apparel world, or even business in general at that point. That was in 2007. I sold my half of that company in 2012, it's still going strong, and my old business partner and I are still buddies. It was a really big learning experience for me, and opened my eyes to how the business world works. After that, I started a kettlebell company in 2010, which I sold four years later. I built up another apparel line in 2013 that I sold a couple years later. Now, at Industry Threadworks, I use what I've learned with my previous businesses to help other companies grow their brand, and make more money with their apparel products."

Like Ryan, I always want to look toward the next obstacle to overcome and the next setback I can emerge from better and stronger than I was before. In other words, I've learned not to let adversity discourage, so much as motivate me.

Another question Maveriqs Academy posed to Ryan focused on how he's dealt with challenges and overcome adversity in his career after serving.

"I use my experiences and lessons learned from having made mistakes, by helping our clients avoid stepping in those same potholes," he responded. "One of my favorite sayings is, 'It's a lot easier, faster, and cheaper to learn from other people's mistakes than to make your own.'

"It's funny to look back to when my business partner and I started our first apparel company. We had no idea how much we didn't know. We had a couple thousands shirts produced. The shirts cost us $15 apiece and we planned to sell them for $25 apiece. We were so sure that we were going to be millionaires making $10 profit per shirt. We didn't realize that the markup on apparel, if you're an efficient apparel company, should be anywhere from 300 to 400 percent, not a 40 percent margin like what we were doing at the time.

"We ended up losing about $70,000 our first year making a bunch of small mistakes like that. Thankfully we learned from each mistake, and never made the same one twice. Eventually we were able to make that company successful and recover from our mistakes even though it cost us a lot of time and money. Mistakes like that have allowed us to be more efficient now, because the things that used to take me ten hours to do, now take me ten minutes to do. I refer to that in some of my videos as gaining 'traction.' You can have all the motivation or horsepower in the world, but if you can't put that power down to the ground and make efficient forward momentum, you're wasting energy and will eventually run out of gas before you reach your destination. Trust me, I love cars and burnouts are cool, but they don't get you anywhere."

But it was Ryan's answer to a question about where he turns for advice himself these days that most intrigued me.

"Number one is people who are doing better than me. People who have been through what I'm going through and know the answers to questions that I have. Again, it's way easier to learn from other people's mistakes than to make your own. It's way cheaper, faster, and more efficient. So I'm always trying to learn from more experienced people as much as possible.

"Another interesting thing is that people will hit me up on Facebook or other social media platforms and ask for advice about business. I've found that by answering those questions I also learn quite a bit on my end. First, I'll learn about the person who asked the question; that's good, direct information across a variety of markets.

Second, it's very true that to truly understand something, you have to teach it.

"By way of answering those questions and teaching others what I know, it helps me organize the information that I have into a cleaner, more effective version. By default, I'm constantly refining my own processes and practices through self-reflection, as well as incorporating various ideas I pick up from the variety of people I talk to across different business models."

In other words, Ryan Williams never rested on his laurels. Every time he achieved something, reached his goal, he turned his attention to the next goal, the next hill to climb, always with humility, knowing that every start offered a new beginning. And he didn't just seize the moment, he has seized *every* moment, a wonderful life lesson rendered even more meaningful by the fact that he is seizing his moments now by helping others seize theirs.

Being confident and being arrogant might seem interchangeable in this respect, but they're not. To paraphrase my SEAL brother Nick Hays, success should never breed complacency or the impression that you have it all and own the top—that's arrogance, while confidence is the desire, above all else, to continue to climb. Confidence turns to arrogance when feelings get in the way of goals, and arrogance is a much bigger wall than adversity. I want to share with you one of those moments for me.

When I was with my platoon and we were deployed and I was doing my job, I finally found a chance to relax, a chance to take it all in and say to myself, "I made it. I have arrived. I'm on top." That was when I slipped up, that was when I needed to get my butt kicked by my brothers. They needed to tell me I wasn't doing all that I could. They needed to tell me that I was not performing to the level of their standards. I was messing up; I wasn't living the way that our SEAL ethos was telling me to. I got sloppy and I got complacent. I needed Gotez to remind me that I was not the answer, that I needed to get back on track, because I was letting the title and the name get to my head. I was not living up to the lofty status that was set before me and that I wanted to uphold.

The reality is that it is very hard to maintain, on some days almost impossible, but it is necessary nonetheless to not get in the way of yourself, because pride comes before the fall. When I was on top, I didn't know how that ruined me until it was almost too late. I'm lucky to have the friends I do who are man enough to tell me when I am wrong, and strong enough to knock me down.

That's love.

Please don't just read through what was just said, or overlook it. Having the humility to take ownership of what you should do instead of pointing your finger to find a scapegoat is the very start of you getting back on track. That's what I did, and that is when things really started to improve for me.

Were things hard? Yes! Was I better for it? Yes.

You have got to realize that when things seem their hardest and aren't going your way, you must find it inside yourself to accept that, and do the things that others wouldn't do. Will you be the one who will give up when it gets harder? Or rise up and train harder and not lose focus on your dreams, and your goals? It seems like an easy answer. Not to be cliché, but it's always easier said than done.

After getting back home I applied the lessons learned from my time overseas, and began to think of the best way that I could help out others who were going to be in my shoes downrange in the months and years to come.

Remember my mention of the Iraqi operative who went by the code name of Johnny Walker? Because of his experience and understanding of the Iraqi culture, I came to him after I was approached by the Foreign Language Program (FLP) to help develop a plan to integrate the best practices, methodologies, and protocols for a speaker of a foreign language. I left the SEAL team for a time and took on an instructor role to help push the FLP in the right direction, working side-by-side with Johnny Walker to make a real difference.

I saw the added value that I brought to the Teams by doing what I did. There was way more than just that role to fill in the job, but the part of teaching and figuring out a way to help others who were in my shoes was very gratifying to me. Teaching others to be better than myself became my ultimate goal. I just wanted guys to evolve, and push past their previously thought limits. My goal was for them to surpass me so that I felt that I made a difference.

I think that explains why the end of active duty for me wasn't an end to my duty at all. I've found that if you teach others what you already know, you keep growing and improving yourself. And encouraging others to do what you can do keeps arrogance out of the picture because your achievements become bigger than yourself. Essentially, every person you steer in the right direction, and bring closer to their goals, becomes a duplicate of yourself. In this sense, you can be taught by the person you're teaching at the same time. Every person I've mentored has made me learn something about myself I didn't know before. As a result, I never stop seeking to improve, to do better and be better.

And there's plenty of room for improvement. Right now, I'm struggling with an aging body that comes complete with a full hip replacement, two shoulder surgeries, and numerous concussions, just to name a few injuries. There are definitely times when I wake up in the morning and I say to myself, *What are you going to do today?* The easiest answer is, "I'm going to sit on this couch and watch TV and think about and plan what I'm going to do!" There's nothing wrong with planning, so long as it doesn't come at the expense of doing. If I make an excuse, instead of pushing forward to represent my community and my God, then in my mind I didn't do everything that I could that day to be the best Me that I can be.

It comes down again to the difference between confidence and arrogance, a crucial distinction in attaining success by not just reaching your goals, but continuing to reach for more. It's not a question of knowing it all, so much as knowing enough. That's one of the great lessons I learned as a SEAL. You're never done, never fully accomplished, never the be-all and end-all. There's always somebody better, somebody smarter, somebody faster, and somebody stronger. If you're among the best at something, it's because you always had someone pushing you to your limits, at the same time you pushed yourself, while never losing touch with humility. That's why BUD/S training breaks you down to the degree that it does: so once you succeed, you'll carry none of the arrogance over the finish line. That's what I love the most about being part of that brotherhood. None of us believes we're any better than the next man, only that we're all better and stronger together as a unit, pushing each other.

Immediately after my EAOS (end of active obligated service), I landed a job with the help of businessman Joe Sweeney and the Honor Foundation set up by Joe Musselman. I really wanted to get to the next phase of life and to get some experience under my belt in the civilian world, a process that started at General Motors, of all places. I found myself thrown into the society of the "normal." The way that everyone else did things, the way that big corporations work, and the way that they think and act. I was on an island of normalcy that made me feel both stranded and lost.

I had people say stuff like, "You did *what*? And you want to work here? What are you going to do, kill me if I get out of line?" And, of course, there were all the usual whispers that "he could kill you with his pen" talk. The truth is I could...but I just wanted to get a taste of the real world.

Truthfully I didn't know what I wanted to do as a civilian. I just knew that after I was done with my military service, I could make a difference in anything I chose to do. I wanted to start my life with my family and be home for my amazing wife and kids. I wanted to use what I learned while being a part of something extraordinary and take that to other areas of life. And at General Motors, I learned far more than I thought I would that helped prepare me for the next phase of my life in which I was to settle.

I worked alongside people who'd been there for a very long time and thought they knew everything. They were unwilling to listen to others and take responsibility for certain things. That kind of culture was the polar opposite of my experience as a SEAL. These General Motors vets thought they were entitled, content with having reached what they perceived to be the top of the food chain. In my mind, this is the very definition of an ordinary mindset.

There was nothing wrong with the way these workers operated or the way they did their job at that company, but most would not change to get better and were comfortable with their lot in life. Everything was about the clock, life lived within the confines of an eight-hour day, as if happiness and fulfillment were timed enterprises. Normal behavior and a normal way of thinking, I know, but one that represents an acceptance of the ordinary and status quo. Fine for some people, but not for me and, I'm sure, not for plenty of the workers alongside me, like Matt, Dave, and Ed, who truly wanted more than just a paycheck but didn't know how to go about getting it.

There is no greater service than to one's country, and coming home from that, along with the experiences that got me there, had made it clear to me that a life punching the clock would be an impossible haul. Accepting that lot, tacitly or otherwise, would effectively be to dismiss or, at least, subjugate everything I'd learned and accomplished. Like leaving my true self behind every day I left for work.

What's the difference between ordinary people and extra-ordinary people? Do extraordinary people have something ordinary people don't? We are all victims of our circumstances, but that doesn't mean we have to be prisoners of them. Working in that General Motors plant crystalized that for me, at the same time it made me realize my lot lay in working alongside people who wanted more out of life than a punch card, who were driven to achieve the way I was and needed help learning how to do it. Making a good and solid living is one of the great gifts of the American Dream, but for those like me, it's not enough, because we're driven to do more.

In 2 Timothy, Paul writes to Timothy to expect the struggle and the pain. Achieving success is part and parcel of that, and the more ambitious your reach, the more pain you'll experience in striving to close your hands around your dream. Rule number one of that dream, as my own experience illustrates, is that a price has to be paid. Nothing comes for free.

It comes down to struggle.

Everyone struggles from time to time, if not more often, and if you've followed my story this far, you know I can relate to what that feels like. In other words, you're not alone. In my life, the definition of struggle was enduring crises I wasn't prepared for when they occurred. I felt like the world was on top of me and I couldn't shake it off. Sometimes I just wanted to throw in the towel and give up, and I came close plenty of times. But I never gave up and just kept fighting until I finally fought my way through.

That's the lesson here. To paraphrase Winston Churchill, where some people see a crisis, I see an opportunity. And the thing about my struggles is that I emerged from each one better and stronger than I was before.

The first thought in that regard is that you can't do it alone. Sure, the primary impetus, the motivation, has to come from within. In my case, though, I had parents and older brother who supported me every step of the way and then my wonderful wife who did the same. I had my original teammates and then my Rollback teammates rallying around me, and the wonderful doctors who put me back together not once, but twice. I wasn't going to listen to people telling me what I couldn't do; I wanted to prove them wrong and I had plenty of help along the way. Even Churchill didn't prevail in World War II on his own, and neither should any of us be expected to in the wars we fight every day.

It comes down to overcoming the obstacles in your way that seem insurmountable at first glance, like vast walls too imposing and impenetrable to scale. So you don't try to crash through all at once; instead, you chip away, a little bit at a time. I had to start from the inside. I had to start with the voice in my head telling me I could do this. I had to block out everything to the contrary, because if I didn't block it out I'd have to deal with doubt, and when doubt becomes pervasive, it's the only voice you can hear. You only fail if you lose sight of your goal and give up. I personally found motivation in all the success stories that inspired me and helped me realize that there were plenty of others who'd overcome far more than I was faced with. The truth of our own predicaments is humbled when measured against what others have been faced with and managed to overcome.

We all have a tendency, at times, to become spectators to our own lives, to watch and wait. But spectating doesn't work when there's something you have to overcome. In Rollback land, for example, I was surrounded by fellow future SEALs who were fighting to overcome the adversity they'd experienced, just as I was. We found purpose in our common bond. Being surrounded by them was the best treatment plan possible, just like, absent of adversity, surrounding yourself with successful people is the surest recipe for success. Little good happens in a vacuum, and the people you want to expose yourself to are those who make you feel better about life in general and yourself in particular.

What are you going to do today that you didn't do yesterday? What are you going to *try* today that you didn't try yesterday?

It would be an interesting exercise to answer those questions in a journal on a daily basis. Wonder what it would look like at the end of the year, how many days would be blank versus how many are filled in.

There are no limits, only plateaus, to go with the peaks and valleys that make up the typical cycles of life. How you deal with both determines your level of happiness, and your level of happiness has a direct bearing on your ability to both overcome and succeed. I was called to serve this country and to push my limits far beyond what any normal person thinks they can accomplish, let alone a crippled boy with one good leg about whom everyone said, "You should try something else," or "Be more realistic," or my all-time favorite, "I know I can't do that, so you don't have a chance."

Where would I be today if I had listened to those people?

"If you're a good person, and establish a good reputation for yourself," Ryan Williams told Maveriqs Academy in that same interview I quoted from earlier, *"good things are going to come your way, and people will get to know who you are."*

In other words, negativity is toxic, poison to your ears. If you hear someone talk in a negative way about your abilities or what goals you have, cut them out of your life like a farmer cuts away dead vines from his crops. Having people to push you is a good thing, as opposed to having people who pull you off course, which is, obviously, a bad thing. All things are possible with the right mentality, work ethic, and through the power of God.

Pastor Mike Murdock, founder of something he calls "prosperity theology," has made a great point in this regard, and with regards to focus. He explains that, "The only reason men fail is broken focus." Pastor Mike uses shooting a gun as a metaphor of life, because it takes focus; you can't just aim and shoot. Success in life is similarly anything but random. It requires practice, training. It's not the work of luck or fortune, at least in the vast majority of cases. And we can extend the metaphor even further: it's one thing to be able to shoot the gun, quite another to hit the target, much less the bull's-eye. So success, in the mind of Pastor Mike, is a progression through stages.

Physical rehabilitation is more quantitative here, because your goals are clearly defined by what's wrong with you and what you have to overcome to get back to where you were. Success in other realms, though, requires an equally clear sense of what you want to accomplish and the steps you intend to take. Let's say your stated goal is to lose weight. Well, then you'd focus on an exercise plan and proper eating habits.

The same set of rules applies when you're trying to become something that no one thinks you can against all odds. Out of 214 guys entering my BUD/S class, only 36 made it through Hell Week, one of them being a once "crippled" boy from Michigan. Was it that I was better than the ones who didn't make it? Faster, stronger, bigger? Not even close. It was because I never lost focus on the goal of becoming a Navy SEAL. I told myself that I was never going to quit, never going to ring that bell. And when I got out of the Navy, I realized that what I really wanted to do with the next stage of my life was to keep others from ringing their metaphorical bells as well.

And here's how I did it.

What You Can Learn from This...

1. I never let someone's voice, or my current circumstances, victimize my mind's mental capacity and ability to overcome the odds that were stacked against me in order to succeed.

2. Quitting is not worth it. All that hard work for what? Just to prove others right about me? No thank you.

3. Chip away at your target, finding a way to get 1 percent better than you were yesterday.

4. I must not lose focus on my goals, both short term and long. If I don't break my focus, I will win.

CHAPTER 14

Reckoning

Michigan, Present Day

There comes a time in our lives when we must tell ourselves to grow up and to take ownership of who we are and how we're going to achieve what we want the most. As I got older, I realized that being a man, and being an adult, are two different things. Once I took the responsibility of being the adult instead of just a man on a mission, my perspective changed.

I began to see what others I looked up to were doing, and noticed that what separated those I emulated from those I didn't was that the ones I emulated were doing what needed to be done when no one else stood up to do it. Individuals who had the integrity to do something the right way, even when no one was looking. In order to move forward, I had to let go of the victimized perspective I realized I was clinging to that had kept me from achieving everything I wanted to.

My first order of business was to untangle the chains and vines that imprisoned me when I returned from serving in Iraq. The door that had been everything in my life had closed, and that only exaggerated every experience, every setback, every success. I'd defined myself for so long by all I needed to overcome in order to get where I wanted to go. Now I was back from that place, the door closed behind me, without the one I knew I was looking for in sight.

It certainly wasn't at General Motors, at least not for me.

You know the old saying, one door closes and another door opens? That's all well and good, unless you can't find that other door. So the first thing I realized was that I needed to figure out where to look. I knew I wanted to help others find their way, as I had found mine. But first I had to find the map and learn the proper signposts that would help guide others to the same lessons I learned, while plotting a path to steer round the obstacles certain to get in the way.

I knew that I was called to help others reach their dreams and goals. The fact that I could no longer serve my brothers in the Teams did not mean that I needed to just sit on the bench or in the crowd cheering them on from afar. I knew that I could make a difference in another way. Becoming the man I am today, I realized that there is always another path to success, even though it isn't the path I thought it would be.

I was sure that I could still help my teammates downrange by doing something else and, even more important, that's what I realized I truly wanted to do. That's how I found myself where I am today, mentoring young men and women to become part of the Naval Special Warfare program in one of a whole spectrum of departments: SEAL, SWCC (Special Warfare Combatant-Craft Crewman), EOD (Explosive Ordnance Disposal), Diver, and Air Rescue. These aspiring candidates want to be part of the greatest team on earth, want to make a difference and defend the freedoms that define our country. I look at these young men and women and see younger versions of myself, eager to serve and prove they can cut it in some of the most challenging programs the entire military has to offer. They need the kind of guidance that can only come from someone who's walked the road down which they want to venture. Their desire is never in question; only whether or not they have the capacity to scale the mental or physical walls that lay ahead of them. My job is to give these candidates the tools they need to complete the climb successfully, thinking the whole time how much

I would've benefitted from being mentored in the way I am now mentoring others.

I was raised by hardworking parents from the baby boomer generation. They understood what it took to make a living and raise a family, their success defined by the levels to which they achieved those goals. They'd overcome so much in striving for these most basic goals, from my brother's death to my own physical impairments. It hadn't been easy for them, but I guess it's not easy for anyone, not really.

I, on the other hand, grew up between generation X and the millennial mindset, embracing neither while being part of both. These generations don't see the world the same way my parents did. Too many of my contemporaries search for more, but end up with less. I wonder if the intrinsic appeal of Donald Trump, the one basic element that brought him to the presidency, was his slogan "Make America Great Again." I'm not even sure he knew what he meant by that, but I think the people it resonated with, older generations that had a different definition for what made America great, definitely knew. And I think, at its core, it embodied a return to the baby boomer mindset in which expectations were different and infinitely more achievable.

We know a lot about so many things, because with the Internet our access to information is limitless. But how much do we really know? In learning a little about a lot of things, it seems we never learn a lot about enough. The experience of simple hard work and forming the values it takes to achieve true success gets lost in the equation.

Sometimes, in other words, less is more.

If you are a millennial, or know more about apps and computers than you do about how to change the oil in your car or build a deck, then this message is for you. If you believe that if you don't reach success it's someone else's fault, then this is for you. If you get angry or have outbursts when things don't go your way, like losing a presidential election and venting your emotions and feelings all over social media platforms, then you are still a child chained by your mindset to politically correct rhetoric that impersonates achievement and accomplishment.

Here's an exercise to consider doing. For one week, keep track of all the time you spend on Twitter, Facebook, texting, and surfing. Then, at the end of the week, make a list of what you accomplished in all that time. Next, make a second list of all the things you could have done with that same time that would have been more productive and left you with something besides tired fingers and thumbs. That perfectly illustrates the principles of the zero-sum game. An hour of texting instead of taking a walk with a friend. An hour on Facebook instead of making your kids turn off their video games and doing something together. And the scariest thing is that in accepting the new way as the new normal, we're breeding a new generation connected far more to their devices than to actual human beings. Remember when voice mail was a big deal? Now, nobody leaves messages anymore and if you want to talk to someone, you text them to call you.

I have a teacher friend who at the beginning of class one day told his eighth-grade students to put all their phones facedown atop their desks, where they wouldn't be allowed to touch or look at them for the entire forty-five minute health class. Remember, this was during school time, and by the end of that forty-five minutes, some of them were literally crawling out of their skin over not being able to follow the world as defined by emojis and 140-word messages.

Is that what the SEAL friends and brothers I've lost over the years fought and died for? Is our culture becoming immune to any message that can't be imparted on a screen, pounded out by a pair of thumbs pressing keys in blinding fashion?

My parents had none of that as part of their world, and I returned from Iraq realizing it wasn't going to help me find the door I was looking for either. So how did I find it exactly?

Training to become, and then serving as, a Navy SEAL is all encompassing because it has to be. Lives, and sometimes even more, are at stake and excuses can't be tolerated any more than distractions. You live in a life bubble that shuts out anything not directly related to the mountain, the river, the operation, the regimen, or the mission ahead. You view everything before you in that context. You are a SEAL, and the next moment commands your focus, and your attention goes no further than the next mission. Your choices are simple and often determined by the very clear demarcation between life and death. You live to live and keep others alive. You serve without pondering the whys, just the whens and wheres. You live for the brothers you've trained with and fight with, because you need them as much as they need you. It's life reduced to its most basic, and fulfilling, tenets.

When I wasn't an active SEAL any longer (notice I said "active"), the world opened up before me in all its scope and sprawl. I didn't know my place anymore, where exactly I fit in. A lot of military veterans, tragically, never find their way after serving. They come away from their service as warriors who are strong, but sometimes broken, and the world contributes to breaking them even more. A staggering twenty-two veterans commit suicide every day. Writing about the causes and ramifications of that would take up an entire book, and I might write it someday.

It's too easy to be bitter about the popular viewpoints of today's culture, one that has demeaned the bold choice the warriors among us make to stand up against evil people on behalf of our country. After so many years of being detached from "real" life, I returned to a culture in which people felt the world owed them something. I was struck by the level of entitlement that permeated our society, too many people believing the world revolved around them and forgetting that winning the rat race doesn't make you any less of a rat.

I call this the WIIFM Effect.

"What's In It For Me?"

It's the first question on the minds of far too many.

Upon returning home, I fell into this mindset and it nearly ruined me, and it will do the same for you. I found myself always looking at the ways in which any situation could be made better for me, instead of finding a way to make things better for others. The WIIFM mindset is a recipe for failure. What changed everything for me was adopting an alternative mindset that focused on earning my way to what I wanted to become.

The sense of entitlement needs to be broken off and put through the meat grinder. Then eat the old you up for breakfast. You must be patient, brothers and sisters. Nothing worth very much comes easy. Like a farmer who waits for the land to yield its valuable crop first has to wait out the spring rains and autumn frosts. You, too, have to be patient and wait out the rains and frosts that fall in your life. Take the time to gain experience, and use the moments where you don't get what you want to mold you and make you stronger, not make you feel like you were cheated.

That's a warrior's creed, applied to everyday life.

The reality I had to come to grips with over and over in my life was that I didn't deserve anything that I didn't earn. I needed to fail time and time again so that I could understand the process of growth, and learn to fail forward, as some people say. In SEAL training, there's an award given out to the Honor Man, usually to the guy who gets it right the first time every time. I didn't get that award, far from it. By no means did I think I should have either. SEAL training didn't come any easier for me than anything else I've achieved in my life, and I'm glad it didn't. I needed to fail first to learn what to do and what not to do. As a man or woman, you should not think you deserve to be the best, unless you outperform and outwork others. No one is entitled to anything.

So don't go on Google and think, *I know it all.* Technology, that maddening millennial social media attachment, is a tool, a means to an end as opposed to an end in itself. You have more access to whatever you want with the technology today to enable you to succeed. Everything you need is, literally, just a click or a download away, providing an easily held misconception that life itself should be that easy. That success and fulfillment itself are just a click away too. In a culture based on instant gratification, it's easy to fool ourselves into believing that the world owes us that simplicity, and we can achieve our goals with the ease of a posting on Snapchat or Instagram.

Uh-uh. Sorry.

The fact that there is an app for everything only makes things easier for you to learn what you need; it doesn't mean that you've earned anything. We're deluged with information to the point where the only way we can deal with it is to fall under the misconception that it's ours to control. The nature of our culture has become pop culture. Our "heroes" have never achieved anything of true merit. They are famous for nothing more than being famous, and we revel in their celebrity to lower our standards for our own lives. Forward thinkers like philosopher Marshall McLuhan and artist Andy Warhol saw this phenomenon coming, but when Warhol famously coined the phrase that in the future everyone would be famous for fifteen minutes, no one really bought into the looming accuracy of the metaphor. We've traded living for real through actual experience, to living vicariously through the experience of pop culture. Think for a minute how the Greatest Generation, members of which are sadly dwindling more and more, would think of this as their legacy. What would they think of a society where everyone who plays wins a trophy regardless of performance, or gets to retake a test in school because they failed it? What would they make of a world where accountability is only what pop culture deems it should be?

Not much, I think.

We need to learn from their example instead of ignoring it. We need to earn our spot, just as they did, and work relentlessly toward what we want, instead of waiting for it to be given to us. Our nation's warriors fought and died for your ability to create your own destiny. Don't squander it based on the superficial ideals championed by a popular culture that crowns the likes of Kim Kardashian and

Justin Bieber. Name me one thing of merit either of them has ever accomplished, or one thing they've done for someone else, to lift someone else up instead of themselves. And these are heroes to so many? Enough said.

When evaluating any situation, I've learned the best thing you can do is take a step back, outside yourself, and then try, as objectively as possible, to see what's before you. Look at things from that angle and as many angles as possible to make the proper assessment and see what you might be missing. But don't confine yourself to strictly your own viewpoint. Research and ask others who've been there and done that. That way, you can make the best, most informed decision based on what lies objectively before you, as opposed to acting rashly or impulsively. I can't tell you how many times I've heard people say, "If only I'd had more time to think." Well, make more time to think. Success and failure, while not predetermined, can be quantified by how much planning and forethought goes into evaluating a situation, and making the most informed decision, based on that assessment. No one consciously chooses to do the wrong thing; everyone believes themselves to be right, that they've chosen the proper path, the proper direction. And the more painstaking and deliberate the decision-making process, the more likely they are to be correct.

In other words, do it right, not rushed. And if you encounter a setback along the way, back up and find another route. Just because life is hard and things don't go your way doesn't make you a failure, unless you quit. When you get knocked down, you have to get right back up and keep pushing, without expecting anyone else to help you. That's how you grow, that's how you can draw the fastest line between where you are and where you want to be.

There's a scene from the Batman movie *The Dark Knight*, where Harvey Dent delivers a line that fits perfectly into a reality we can all relate to. He was talking about how Caesar was elected the leader of his nation, after returning to Rome a hero, only to give in to all manner of ego and hubris in an incessant attempt to expand his power. To paraphrase Dent's thinking on this, you either die a hero or live long enough to become the villain. I would add to that, *if you're not careful*. Why? Because of the overriding tendency to believe we're above it all and better than everyone else, when both are actually very seldom true.

When you're not careful, when you let hubris and the WIIFM mindset take control, you risk negatively affecting not just yourself, but also others. Your family, your coworkers, and your friends. One of the primary lessons about being a SEAL that can be applied to everyday life is that the team comes first. As individual SEALs we exist to serve a greater good. And we can only complete our mission successfully by harking back to all those lessons in BUD/S training. In the Boats on Heads drill, if one person falters, the boat comes down. In failing, you hurt not only yourself, but everyone around you.

As soon as you view yourself as the victim in your own life, metaphorically you bring the boat down on everyone. Instead of complaining about the circumstances that define our lives, we have to make the best of them and take ownership. Don't complain, act. Ask yourself what can I do to make today better than yesterday. And if every day is better than the day before...

I'm reminded again of Marcus Luttrell tossing a stone a few yards ahead of him over and over again, in working his broken body down that mountain in Afghanistan. I'm reminded of how great the feat of simply getting myself from the couch to the bathroom felt to a little boy in leg braces. Small victories may not seem like much at the time, but their sum total can have a drastic impact on your life.

The challenge lies in seeing how things truly are, not how you want them to be or how they appear on Twitter, Facebook, Instagram, or Snapchat. Relying on appearances molded by others to craft your existence is the moral equivalent of letting others live your life for you. We all know the positive attributes of social media, but the negative side can be far more destructive and pervasive. I see this all the time with the hopeful SEAL candidates I now mentor. They're more comfortable being on a device and validating their feelings from social media, than they are explaining to me what their issues are and how I can help them. They would rather look up an answer or search for a "how to" than ask me the same question, as if the detachment of a machine lessens the vulnerability stoked by human interaction. Having the answer to any question a Google search away muddles the distinction between knowledge and thought. They can learn what they need without thinking.

And yet too often they're afraid to look me in the eye, because they are intimidated by another man who doesn't seek out self-recognition or validation from a sympathetic group of fans or followers. The comfort of strangers just really isn't worth very much in my mind, almost as if growing up doesn't necessarily mean they grow out of this reliance on relationships with people they never have to meet. One of my chief admonitions for these fledgling SEALs I'm responsible for mentoring and preparing is to place their value in people instead of posts, pictures, and profiles. And that's a lesson all of us can learn from, since I don't think anybody betters themselves, or finds true enrichment, in 140 characters or less.

What also disturbs me, and is a clear recipe against self-improvement, is using social media to lash out at someone you work with or work for. This is cowardly and destroys any progress that could be made by going to that person and actually talking to them. Ask yourself when was the last time that happened. When was the last time you actually talked out your differences instead of posting them and, likely, irrevocably damaging the relationship? Once something is said in public, it's out there forever. You can't take it back. There's a reason why it's called a "private" life, but too many people today seem averse to anything that even resembles private, as if they find some form of affirmation in informing their followers of every bit of minutia in their lives. I find the whole notion of being a "Facebook friend" to be an oxymoron.

Everyone's looking for shortcuts, to find friends and even romance without having to work at it on an interpersonal level. In addition to the principle of What's In It For Me, there's this obsession with instant gratification; that if it doesn't come fast, it's not worth pursuing at all. That's the antithesis to what I learned in training to become a SEAL. And well before then, I realize now it was a blessing that so much came so hard for me as a young boy. I learned to appreciate the things everyone else takes for granted.

There's no app that can guarantee success overnight, or in a day, a week, a month, and maybe even a year or longer. But there is a formula.

What You Can Learn from This…

1. Look out and see what you can do for others, Once I did this more and more doors open for even better opportunities. (Thank you, Joe Sweeny.)

2. Just because I know something, doesn't mean I shouldn't listen to what my elders tell me. To know, but not to do, is not to know. (Stephen R Covey)

3. Your goals in life must be made through the hardest of work, and mastered by your time and efforts, not by downloading an app or searching online, but by living the grind and pushing past your comforts.

CHAPTER 15

Victim or Hero

Michigan, Present Day

You can either make yourself the victim in your story or the hero. It really is up to you. Your mindset must change, and you must not believe that anybody owes you something. Improving yourself, and your immediate circle, is a conscious decision. For me it comes down to a choice between serving God, or becoming, in essence, your own god and worshipping yourself and what you create. I can say that because, as you've seen from my experiences, I've been on both sides, and part of the reason I wanted to write this book was to educate others on the distinction, so they choose the right path.

Throughout my life I've been tested by this battle, as much as the ones I fought in Iraq with my SEAL brothers, and now I can discern what is the will of God, what is good and acceptable in His eyes. I am by no means perfect and will never claim to be. I will never claim to be better than you or above anyone. I do, however, believe that I've been given the wisdom that may be despised because of its exclusiveness, and that's okay with me. Once I put to death what belonged to my selfish nature, I was able to see the truth. I was no longer a prisoner of false choices between equally detrimental decisions. Instead of looking outward toward an impersonal approach to life lived behind a computer screen, I learned to look inward toward renewing my own mind and spirit.

In that respect, the end of active duty for me proved to be just the beginning of my service. As a SEAL mentor, training Naval Special Warfare candidates, I see the whole gamut of individuals with a burning desire to be part of NSW or to become a SEAL. Generally speaking, they all start out one of two ways: They have the will, but are not physically ready. Or they're in great physical shape, but lack the mental toughness.

In my mind, the first option is infinitely preferable in terms of my ability to succeed as a mentor. If a candidate possesses all the will and desire, he can overcome the physical issues and hardships holding him back, just as I did on more than one occasion. As in my case, it takes dedication, discipline, and hard work to master the physically demanding skills required to be a SEAL. Candidates can achieve the physical gains they need to make with time spent in the gym or pool. Measure the time well spent in incremental gains, since nothing worthwhile is ever accomplished overnight. Because in the long run there is no better teacher than failure. If I make a SEAL candidate I'm mentoring fail over and over for weeks and weeks, but they come back harder and stronger, then I know that I have a solid prospect on my hands.

Which brings me to the second group, those with the physical, but not necessarily mental, wherewithal to make it. Candidates like this inevitably excel until they face adversity, something like treading water in the pool with a brick, and have no idea how to respond. They haven't failed or been challenged enough to react properly. Things have come too easily for them for too long, and they look at becoming a SEAL the way they did trying out for school sports team when nobody could be cut. Having everyone regardless of their record winning trophies, merely for participating in youth sports, may be politically correct, but it represents a mindset that is antithetical to achieving success in a real-world environment.

And training to become a SEAL is a *hyper*–real-world environment where you know going in how much the odds are stacked against you and how hard you'll have to work to overcome them.

The problem is too many of the candidates I mentor *don't* know that, because the odds have never really been stacked against them. They made every team they ever tried out for, won trophies even when they lost, and got to retake every school test they ever failed. Well, there are no do-overs in battle, or SEAL training, and in this case both serve as apt metaphors for life. I push the candidates I mentor, because I want to challenge them in ways they've never really been challenged before, and the latter group seldom responds well to that. Nor do they come to the realization that they even need to change. The mental fortitude to persevere when times get tough and things go wrong seems to be missing from their psyches. When they are faced with losing, or failing, they blame others—mainly me—and aren't willing to accept defeat when others outperform them. They want to point at others for being responsible for their failure, instead of pointing the finger at themselves. They lack not just humility, but also accountability, and it's my job as a SEAL mentor to give them both. It's what I learned from my own experiences and what I hope this book imparts to you.

Being a SEAL isn't just a lifestyle; it's also a metaphor for how we all can live our lives, even absent of military service. Warriors continue to fight battles long after they've hung up their weapons, and those battles often serve the community. For me, it's showing the next generation of potential Navy SEALs the way. For another of my brothers, Andy Stumpf, it's something else entirely, as he writes about here:

> This amazing nation is protected by volunteers willing to write a check to the United States of America for an amount up to, and including their lives. When that check is cashed, the destruction left behind is almost beyond description.

Behind every soldier serving in our military is a family whose love and support makes their complete and unwavering commitment to this country possible. When those families receive notification that a husband, father, or son are gone, they need all that love and support given right back.

Since retiring from the military it's been a persistent and painful struggle to watch the fight from the sidelines. Even though I can't physically go overseas and contribute, I refuse to sit back and do nothing. I've decided to put it all on the line to support the Navy SEAL community and their families who live with their toes on the line everyday.

My goal is to set four world records in one jump to raise 1 million dollars to fund the Navy Seal Foundation Survivor Support Program for 2016.

What a world it would be if everyone had the inclination to give back in ways big, like Andy with his record-breaking wingsuit jumps, as well as small. Unfortunately, though, not everyone possesses that inclination, not even close, and that leaves us to question the value judgments that are made when categorizing people. This really dawned on me upon reading a June 2016 blog written by Andy that offered a fresh take on the old folk tale about sheep, sheepdogs, and wolves. His words resonated with me in a way that leaves me quoting Andy verbatim instead of trying to paraphrase him, so here's his blog:

> I am sure everyone has heard the fable of the sheep, sheepdog, and the big bad wolf. It is used to describe categories of humans, and I am certain it is wrong.
>
> Sheep crave a wall, because others tell them physical barriers provide protection. The sheep face inward from the wall, and keep their head down. Sheep are constantly told by others that the wall makes them safe, and they cannot live without it.
>
> Sheepdogs appreciate a wall, but they do not require it. Sheepdogs spend the majority of the day facing outward, but they do not stray too far from the wall, or the flock. Their vision, and the distance they can see into the "outside" world, has limits. Sheepdogs are

sharp, they question what they hear, and make informed decisions tempered by real life experiences. The sheepdog has a capacity for violence, but a respect for life, and love for his flock.

The wolf sees the entire world. He lives outside of the walls, maneuvering, searching, and observing multiple flocks. He can manipulate entire ecosystems with his actions, or lack thereof.

The wolf realizes that a wall can serve many purposes. It can be a threat because it can limit access to food. It can also be a weapon. The wolf can manipulate the sheep into building bigger and bigger walls, until all of their freedoms are surrendered in the name of security. Eventually that facade crumbles and the sheep are exposed, physically and mentally unprepared. Easy targets.

The wolf is violent. He attacks with sharp teeth, does not shy away from being aggressive, and does not apologize for who he is. If knocked down, the wolf does not tuck tail and run, he gets back up and attacks with vigor. The wolf lives on the fringe, at the edge of what is possible.

The reason the wolf is made out to be the villain is the same reason our society is headed in the wrong direction. We would rather deny the fact that sharp teeth even exist, in the hopes of offending no one, than take the time to justify their occasional use.

Be whoever you want to be, and do whatever you want to do, just don't do it with a blindfold on.

The most dangerous animal in the fable, and the most dangerous person in the real world, is a sheep.

Andy Stumpf and I share a lot of the same beliefs, foremost among them being that when you see the world the way we have, the nature of truth itself becomes abundantly clear. The battle in life isn't just an earthly one, but also a spiritual one we can be prepared for when an enemy, metaphorical or otherwise, strikes. We must be prepared by not giving into the illusion that there is no enemy, there is no hardship, and everything will take care of itself in the end, just like we don't have to win anymore to get a trophy. Too often we see only the high-gloss finish, and we don't peer closer to see the mars, dings, and imperfections that lurk beneath it.

Combat, you see, is an apt metaphor for life itself. Must we mourn another tragic defeat and turn our view strictly inward, ignoring the wolves lurking outside our walls who move freely through the lands waiting to attack with malice and hate? How did we stray from God as the cornerstone of our country, our faith, and our life? Maybe because He wasn't the one giving out all those trophies.

Martin Luther King, Jr. said light is the only thing that drives out darkness. Generation Y, or millennials, need to see what's wrong with them and stop blaming others for their problems and defeats. I tell you this because that was me. I shared this mindset with countless others, and all it did was keep me from success and from reaching my full potential.

I'd like to share a list of what's pervasive in this mindset that I wish someone had shared with me to guide me toward the proper path I missed far too often along the way. So in no particular order...

Winner Take Nothing: Having everyone get the sense that they've won, even when they lose, lessens the value of achievement and sends a terrible message to children about the future. Our culture has become so loss-adverse, it would prefer to leave kids thinking that they're going to win all the time, a mindset that reduces the impact of practice and preparation. With winning and losing no longer black and white, they live their lives in a nebulous gray zone of lower standards that hardly equips today's young people for the demands and challenges of the real adult world. Upon entering that world, they're destined to face the rude awakening that they are not the be-all and end-all. That the sheep's wool has been blinding their eyes to the truth, that their specialness is in their own mind and adults don't get trophies for just showing up.

Deserving It All: A sense of entitlement is what you foster with a generation that feels life is not just there for the taking, it's there to be served up to them on a silver platter. In many ways, this is the most destructive and counterintuitive cultural trend on my list, since it devalues achievement and accomplishment. It's the moral equivalent of coasting through BUD/S training, because you know you're going to make it and become a SEAL, regardless of your performance. It breeds a "going through the motions" mentality, and even that might be giving too much credit where it's not due.

Me First, Second, and Third: All you think about is yourself and what's in it for you. All that you do in life is in pursuit of self-gratification, and you don't care who gets in your way or who you negatively affect in the process. This is an offshoot of the What's In It For Me philosophy and represents the antithesis of everything the SEAL ethos stands for.

Why Fight When You Can Quit: If something's hard, why bother doing it? If you're not good at something, don't bother with it, right? Wrong. I saw the following on the Bright Side Facebook page (yes, I do use social media as a tool!):

When a child is learning how to walk and falls fifty times, they never think to themselves, "Maybe this wasn't for me."

I find that to be an apt metaphor when it comes to giving up. The small percentage of my fellow SEALs who successfully made it through BUD/S training refused to quit, refused to accept failure. I think life can sometimes be boiled down to a simple question: Do you want to be one of the ones who stays or goes? Take the challenge to do your best at the things you are not good at and rise to the challenge by training harder and putting in more time than you want to.

An Age-Old Problem: As a professional mentor, I'm struck by how millennials, Gen Y, seek so little guidance from those who've been there and done that already. They seem to think they can do it better, that old thinking needs to be updated for its own sake, so why bother asking an elder for help? They have the attitude that they already know everything, so what's an elder going to teach them? Seeking out guidance means admitting that you don't know as much as you wish you did. But that doesn't mean you won't, eventually, if you take the time to try. It's possible on this earth that when other people tell you something, they actually may know more than you. Just because you can look it up on YouTube or Wikipedia doesn't mean you know how to do it or that you are more proficient than another.

Those are things I'd tell my younger self, if I could. And I'd tell myself something else too:

Have grit.

I'd define grit the same way Mark Twain famously did when he wrote, "It's not the size of the dog in the fight, it's the size of the fight in the dog." You can plug in all manner of clichés here, but the bottom line is that fighting for something lends it meaning. The means to an end can become an end in itself, because even if you don't win the first time, it doesn't mean you won't win the next. Having grit means learning from your mistakes and not being afraid to recognize the need to learn from someone who's better than you at it. You can persevere through all the negative and all the losses to reach your long-term goals—that's the very definition of finding your way.

No one is born successful. The best we can hope is to be born with the tools that enable us to become a success. If you are trying to become a Navy SEAL, or pursuing any other elite title or career, then like me you must realize that this something that has to be earned every day—in the gym, in books, everywhere; in understanding that climbing a mountain takes a long time, and may cause you to double back and take a different path to the top. But the view from there will make it all worthwhile once you arrive, especially when you're looking down at all the others who gave up because it was too long or too hard.

I want you to have the right mindset and belief in yourself. Believe that you can do anything if you have the drive and are willing to work hard enough. Dreams are just that until you make them come true. You have to be patient, yes, but not at the expense of the sense of urgency that should always be driving you. "Blink and you'll miss it," is an apt description of life, and you don't want to blink.

You want to move forward and grow with your eyes wide open and focused on the target in your sights.

I don't know how old you are, but it doesn't matter because I'm here to tell you that you still have time, that now is the time. There is no greater or more opportune moment than now. So let's get after it and not surrender to what others tell you is impossible. Apply the life lessons you've developed yourself, or learned from others, and start forward along a path to what you want the most.

What You Can Learn from This...

1. Own it: plain and simple. Sometimes you have to do the things you don't want to do to get what you want.

2. Have the grit to get past the uncomfortable feeling of pain and loss and failure to take the next step forward.

3. No one will do the work for you, but you. There is no easy way to the top of a mountain, that's why people are always looking up from afar, while you could be looking out from the top.

Bigger Than Myself

You may believe that someone like me, who has overcome life's obstacles to find success, can give you the keys to finding your way in life as well.

You may be able to relate to me and understand pain and loss. We may have a bond or a similar path that led us to this point. You may believe that, like me, you have the ability to overcome the odds.

I told you my life's history not to boast, but to let you know that dreams can come true, so long as you bleed long enough and have the grit to grind and carve out the path that may not be visible to anyone but you.

I have spoken to many people across the United States and shared with them my testimony on how I had to overcome odds that were stacked against me, told cool stories of how it all went down, and described what I learned from my situation. I tell them the story of overcoming adversity and what it means to be resilient. I show them that it's possible, even though it's hard, but that they can do it. I give them the right mindset to take home, something that no one can take away from them.

When I speak, people see that I have added value to their lives, and that I am not there just to entertain them. I'm not there just because I'm a Navy SEAL and they want to hear cool war stories. I can talk to them without them dismissing what I have to say. They respect me for what I do and what I have done. They know that I don't ask them to do anything that I haven't done, or am willing to do, myself. I'm there because they need to hear what has to be said in order for them to change, or the mindset of the entire company needs to change, or the whole sports team's mentality must change.

I come by myself, or with my team, to say the hard things and to do what others can't. I make things uncomfortable, and that's the secret because that's where change and growth start to happen, when you're fed up with being at the bottom or a place in your life you don't want to be. Scott Michael, a very successful executive in the Amway Corporation, once said people can only embrace true change, "when you're sick and tired of being sick and tired." When you've tried all the wrong ways to achieve what you want the most, and now you're ready to try something different.

Like motivational speaker Les Brown says, "It's hard, but it's necessary, and when life throws you to the ground, learn to land on your back, because when you can look up you can get up." I say similar things to my men, like "learn to fail forward." If you land on your face be sure you're falling forward, because at least it means you're headed in the right direction.

There is much to find out about yourself throughout this process, but for me it has become more than finding myself. It's become much more about helping people find themselves and success in what they do, helping them achieve greatness. I have found it much more gratifying to make someone else better than I could ever be. When I do that, then I know I am doing right, paying it forward, and showing others a different mindset to success by mapping out directions along a different road, a detour to get them where they want to go.

Out of all the companies I have spoken with and developed a real-life relationship with, one bond in particular stands out above the rest, because of my own life history marked by trying to be the best and failing, bleeding, and crying. I have the honor to have forged a bond and friendship with Coach Erik Spoelstra and the Miami Heat NBA organization. Throughout my professional relationship with him and his basketball team, I've learned just how hard it is to lead in areas beyond the special ops military bubble that I have been surrounded by. It has let me see the parallels to great minds thinking alike and that even such great minds and great athletes sometimes need help too. That we are all human, that we all have faults and that even the greatest of the greats fail at times. That's when they seek out the new perspective, the fresh way of thinking I strive to provide them from my own experiences.

Like you're looking for that new perspective right now, by reading this book. I'd like to help you find your way, as much as I've strived to for Navy SEAL candidates, professional athletes, and corporate types. All I ask is that you keep an open mind and accept that there's always room for improvement. It could be as simple as opening up to another person or admitting when you need help. None of us is invulnerable or impervious to human error. That's why learning to understand the process of growth through, or out of, failure at some points in your life is a great teaching tool to help you succeed, instead of resigning yourself to the fact that your lot in life now will be your lot in life forever.

It has been more than humbling to talk to someone like Erik Spoelstra, a professional basketball coach and, as a Navy SEAL, to see how similar we are and what makes us tick, as well as what motivates us to do better. It's great to be around those at the top of their game (literally, in this case!). When you have the chance to soak it in, you must always be willing to listen and learn, but never to be afraid of the challenge of what lies in front of you, because if you stand among giants, you have the chance to become one. You have to prove it to yourself by earning that spot every day, every time, and every play, because there's always someone as good, or just a little bit better, looking for the same edge you are.

I had the opportunity recently to meet fellow SEAL Jeremiah Patrick Dinnell, aka JP Dinnell. He's built a consulting business called Never Settle, a brilliant life lesson in its own right. I so enjoyed watching how Jeremiah works and learning from him. Going into every meeting and pursuing every contact, charging ahead and living life, never settling for anything and always striving for everything.

And, if it wasn't for my brother from another mother, Remi Adeleke, I know I would not be who I am today. We suffered through the lowest stages of life at the same time as Rollbacks, both physically and spiritually, but his leadership and his love of God pulled him out of the depths of hell and back into life here on earth to thrive. He was my light in the darkest of places when I needed it the most. He is a man amongst men and he is the reason why I've enjoyed the success I have, and am where I am, today. He introduced me to the Acumen Performance Group, or APG, which has worked miracles for professional organizations, ranging from corporate entities to the NFL's Atlanta Falcons, who want to apply the SEAL ethos, standards, and work ethic to their lives and goals. A true SEAL motto is, "The only easy day was yesterday." And once athletic teams and businesses, both large and small, adopt that philosophy, tomorrow gets easier to deal with for them.

APG became a proving ground for me, a means by which I could hone my craft and cement my desire, as well, to teach and mentor others who'd ventured down the same path I'd taken. And for those companies and teams I worked with, I always stressed that for SEALs, the nature of brotherhood continues after serving, because you can reach out to anyone in the community for help, knowing that if you ever need something, they'll be there. It was this very mindset that could help transform a decent company or team into a good one, and a good one into a great one. APG's motto is, "Embrace the suck," something I could relate to all too well, because it spoke to the whole notion of overcoming adversity. Most of those who retained APG's services did so because they wanted to improve performance and had no idea how to change the culture in order to do that. Toward that end, they wanted to experience what it's like to be a SEAL and how we operate, so that they may become as elite in the world of business, or sports, as we are in ours. Learn how to apply SEAL standards and values to their own lives.

Remi also introduced me to Kevin Kent. Some say Kevin is a super-SEAL, whose become the kind of "movie" face for our community, appearing in such films as *13 Hours* and the TNT televisions show, *The Last Ship*. But I know that he's actually far more than that, including a wonderful father and husband. Then there's the very humble Harry Humphries, a legend in the SEAL community, who has paved the way for guys like me to have the introduction into films and opened up doors for many others in their new careers. That led to my opportunity to appear as a credited cast member in the greatest Transformers movie of all time, *Transformers 5*, which will hit theaters right around the time this book is released. (Not something that was planned on purpose, I promise!)

Thanks to Harry and Kevin, that experience placed me alongside actors Josh Duhamel, Santiago Cabrera, and, of course, the film's star, Mark Wahlberg. These guys were great to work with, so down to earth and very funny off set. Surprisingly and perfectly human, just like everybody else. Not arrogant or any of the other Hollywood stereotypes. They showed up on set every day ready to work, and even put in time in the gym with us SEALs before we actually started filming so they could better play their parts. I can't tell you what a blast (no pun intended!) I had working with them, another opportunity I received as a result of being a Navy SEAL, and do I need to remind you of how much I had to overcome to get there? My point being that what all that work did for me in my life continues to pay dividends.

I also spent time studying the film's director, Michael Bay, and learned that all of the chaos everyone always talks about with him and his movies is just a normal thing to a Team Guy. Being successful isn't about avoiding chaos in your life, it's about learning how to deal with and prosper from it. All of the Team Guys I was with on set just thought it was cool that there were other people out there like us who say things and do things the way we do to get the job done, since making a film as big as *Transformers 5* is truly like a top-down military operation. While some may view this as hostile or bizarre, or maybe even crazy, for me it's just another day at work with the people I am so blessed to be around. See, it doesn't matter what the venue is. True hardworking people all want the same thing and are working toward the same goal. That's what I took away from my experience with Michael Bay on the *Transformers 5* set. What normal person gets to do all of this and have the chances that I had and continue to have?

Am I any different than you, or do you have gifts that are better than mine?

The answer is yes to both.

The truth is you are better than me, and you have better gifts than I do, but maybe I outwork you just as others outwork me.

As I work hard to set new goals and reach higher, I understand that I've gotten to where I am because I found the right roads to get me there, either through maps drawn by others or by myself with the guidance of others. And it's not just about getting to the end of that big road and finding what you were looking for. Not at all. It's also about starting down a different road right away to achieve your next goal. Because if you reach the destination that your old goal set you toward, but don't develop new ones, you won't grow, you won't learn, and you won't be any better.

All that I need to do every day is not settle for what life has in store for me at the moment, and to trust God that his plan is better than mine.

If I just sit and wait for something to come along, then nothing will happen, and if I complain about my circumstances instead of making the reality that I want, I will always be looking for a handout and never accomplish anything anymore in my life. No less of a source than Thomas Jefferson had written that, "Nothing can stop the man with the right mental attitude from achieving his goal; nothing on earth can help the man with the wrong mental attitude."

While I can't count Jefferson among those who've had the most direct influence on me, I've had the pleasure of seeing people for who they are and finding true friendships that are formed by the common bond of going through life during the worst of the worst. I have learned that true friendships are ones that are made when you give all that you have to another, expecting nothing in return, but getting back more than you could ever expect. Being a part of the SEAL brotherhood is beyond an honor and I fail forward every day trying to be the best example that I can to make my brothers proud of what I do and whom I represent.

As a wandering man searching for his faith, I only found it once I lost everything that I thought was imperative, and once I gave up my own personal desires for the everlasting life that Jesus Christ provides for me. I am that man, and I am a Christian, and I will continue to be the rock that my family needs me to be, and the mentor that people can come to when they need help, guidance, or just a friend. I will shine in the darkness and love my brothers with all of my heart until it beats its last. I pray that I can pave the way for others to take what I have learned from this life so far, and give them the hope, the belief, and the mindset that all things are possible. Just because they haven't happened yet doesn't mean they won't, especially if you're willing to work as hard as it takes to make them happen.

I know that you can stand up, be strong, and stand firm against the tides of life when the waves crash down on you, by believing in yourself even when no one else does.

You can.

You *will*.

Remember, NO SURRENDER!